A COMPENDIUM
OF THE
RAJA YOGA PHILOSOPHY:

COMPRISING THE PRINCIPAL TREATISES OF SHRIMAT SANKARACHARYA AND OTHER REKNOWNED AUTHORS

TOOKARAM TATYA

GYAN

Published by

Gyan Publishing House
5, Ansari Road
Daryaganj, New Delhi-110002
Phone: 011-47034999, 9811692060
E-mail: books@gyanbooks.com

Distribution Network
gyanbooks.com
India, USA, Canada, UK, Australia

ISBN: 978-93-6920-364-2 (HB)

First Published, 1901

2nd Impression 2025

Printed at: Gyan Press, Delhi.

A COMPENDIUM OF THE RAJA YOGA PHILOSOPHY
Author: TOOKARAM TATYA

Theosophical Publication Fund Series.

A COMPENDIUM

OF THE

RAJA YOGA PHILOSOPHY,

COMPRISING THE PRINCIPAL TREATISES OF
SHRIMAT SHANKARACHARYA AND OTHER
RENOWNED AUTHORS.

FOR THE

BOMBAY THEOSOPHICAL PUBLICATION FUND,

BY

RAJARAM TOOKARAM

1901.

TABLE OF CONTENTS.

PREFACE.

It is in the hope of laying before aspirants to spiritual knowledge, both in the East and the West, particularly before those who do not know Sanscrit, the theory of the Higher self and the mode of its realization that the book is published. It contains English Translations of a few celebrated treatises on the subject :—

1. Sankaracharya's Aparokshanubhuti (Direct cognition of the Unity of Jiva and Brahma).
2. Sankaracharya's Atmanatma Viveka, setting forth the scope and purpose of the Vedanta philosophy.
3. Shri Vakyasudha, teaching the annihilation of egoism to realize the Universal Atma.
4. Vedánta Sára of Sadanand Swami giving a short resumé of the Vedanta philosophy.
5. Sankaracharya's Crest Jewel of wisdom.
6. Charpat Panjari.

We venture to assure our readers that a careful study of these treatises will lead them to an exalted state of the mind which will raise them above the sphere of physical sorrows and pains and ultimately enable them to overcome the limitation of time and space by realizing the Immortal Ego.

अपरोक्षानुभूति

DIRECT COGNITION

OF THE

UNITY OF JĪVA AND BRAHMA

BY

S'RIMAT S'ANKARĀCHĀRYA WITH NOTES
TRANSLATED BY LATE

MANILAL NABUBHAI DVIVEDI, F. T. S.

ॐश्रीहरिं परमानंदमुपदेष्टारमीश्वरम् ।
व्यापकं सर्वलोकानां कारणं तं नमाम्यहम् ॥ १ ॥

1. I* bow to S'ri Hari†—to Is'var—the highest happiness, the best instructor, the all-pervading, the one cause (material instrumental as well as final) of the Universe.

अपरोक्षानुभूतिर्वै प्रोच्यते मोक्षसिद्धये ।
सद्भिरेव प्रयत्नेन वीक्षणीया मुहुर्मुहुः ॥ २ ॥

2. Hence forward is expounded the course of realising the Invisible, for the easy acquisition of final absolution (from the bonds forged by ignorance–*avidyâ*) ; let those only who have sufficiently prepared themselves for being initiated into the secrets of this Science, by every effort frequently meditate upon the truths herein inculcated.

---

* The ego—the *as'uddha jiva* (6th principle) as it were contemplates upon *Ishwar—Brahma*—the creator and yet—the destroyer of all *avidyâ*—ignorance, i. e. tries to realise its primal identity with *Brahma*.

† He who by the light of knowledge *takes* away, *melts* away all *avidyâ*—the common substratum of the three States of sleep, dream and waking.

स्ववर्णाश्रमधर्मेण तपसा हरितोषणात् ।
साधनं प्रभवेत्पुंसां वैराग्यादिचतुष्टयम् ॥ ३ ॥

3. Indifference (1) and the other (3) preliminary qualifications are acquired by the performance of duties peculiar to one's own caste and creed, by austerities, and by propitiating the deities &c.*

ब्रह्मादिस्थावरांतेषु वैराग्यं विषयेष्वनु ।
यथैव काकविष्ठायां वैराग्यं तद्धि निर्मलम् ॥ ४॥

4. That is pure Indifference which consists in the loss of all desire for the enjoyments of the senses, beginning from the *Satyaloka* (the highest heaven) to the *Martyaloka* (this world), as for the dung of a crow.

नित्यमात्मस्वरूपं हि दृश्यं तद्विपरीतगम् ।
एवं यो निश्चयः सम्यग्विवेको वस्तुनः स वै ॥५॥

5. The determination that the only eternal and permanent principle of the Cosmos is *Atman* (the *Subject* of all perception), and that every thing else is opposed in its very nature to this *Atman* (i. e. is unpermanent) as being the object† of perception—Such fixed (theoretical determination, the cause of *Indifference*, is called the Right *knowledge* (2) of objects.

---

*अधिकारी तु विधिवदधीतवेदवेदांगत्वेनापाततोऽधिगताखिलवेदार्थोऽस्मिञ्जन्मानि जन्मान्तरे वा काम्यनिषिद्धवर्जनपुरःसरं नित्यनैमित्तिकप्रायश्चित्तोपासनानुष्ठानेननिर्गतनिखिलकल्मषतया नितांतनिर्मलस्वांतःसाधनचतुष्टयसंम्पन्नः प्रमाताधिकारी ॥ ॥ वेदान्तसार ॥ also

मेधावी पुरुषो विद्वानूहापोहविचक्षणः । अधिकार्यात्मविद्यायामुक्तलक्षणलक्षितः ॥
विवेकिनो विरक्तस्य शमादिगुणशालिनः। मुमुक्षोरेव हि ब्रह्मजिज्ञासायोग्यतामता ॥
॥ विवेकचूडामणिः ॥

† Compare Vákya Sudhá 1.

सदैव वासनात्यागः शमोऽयमिति शब्दितः ।
निग्रहो बाह्यवृत्तीनां दम इत्यभिधीयते ॥ ६ ॥

6. Now the effects (3) of *Indifferences* :—*S'ama, Dama* and four others. The abandonment of all *previous impressions* maturing themselves into tangible effects *now* (*i. e. the controlling* of the *Antaskarana*) is called *S'ama* (1); complete restraint over the bent of the external senses (over our bodily acts) is called *Dama* (2).

विषयेभ्यः परावृत्तिः परमोपरतिर्हि सा ।
सहनं सर्वदुःखानां तितिक्षा सा शुभा मता ॥ ७ ॥

7. The entire turning away from all objects of sense, the almost voluntary absence of all desire for such objects, is the height of *Uparati* (3); and the patient suffering of all pain or sorrow is the state of happy *Titikshâ** (4).

निगमाचार्यवाक्येषु भक्तिः श्रद्धेति विश्रुता ।
चित्तैकाग्र्यं तु सल्लक्ष्ये समाधानमिति स्मृतम् ॥ ८॥

8. Faith in the words of the Upanishads, as well also in the words of those who interpret them—the teachers, (as also, and perhaps chiefly, in one's self)—is called *S'raddhâ* (5); the absorption of the mind in the one paramount aim of all exertion—the *Sat*—the Universal *Atman*—(i. e., excessive desire, *to know* and *realise* that *Paramâtman*; or the utter incapability arising from such a state, of deviating from the right path) is called *Samâdhâna* (6).

संसारबंधनिर्मुक्तिः कथं मे स्यात्कदा विधे ।
इति या सुदृढा बुद्धिर्वक्तव्या सा मुमुक्षुता ॥ ९ ॥

9. When and how shall, oh my Fate, I be free from the bonds of this world—birth and rebirth—this strong and all absorbing desire constitutes the fourth and last of the four preliminary stages—*Desire of Absolution* (4).

* "The cessation of desire, a constant readiness to part with every thing in the world"—Theosophist Vol. V. No. 12. P. 282.

उक्तसाधनयुक्तेन विचारः पुरुषेण हि ।
कर्तव्यो ज्ञानसिध्यर्थमात्मनः शुभमिच्छता ॥१०॥

10. One who having passed through the said preliminary stages desires *knowledge* for final absolution must set himself seriously *to think.*

नोत्पद्यते विनाज्ञानं विचारेणान्यसाधनैः ।
यथा पदार्थभानं हि प्रकाशेन विना क्वचित् ॥११॥

11. Knowledge is not produced by any means other than right thinking; just as the objects of this universe are never perceived but by the help of light.

कोहं कथमिदं जातं को वै कर्त्ताऽस्य विद्यते ।
उपादानं किमस्तीह विचारः सोयमीदृशः ॥१२॥

12. (*a*) Who am I? (*b*) How is this evolved? (*c*) Who is its creator? (*d*) What is the material of which it is made?—This is the form of rational thought.

नाहं भूतगणो देहो नाहं चाक्षगणस्तथा ।
एतद्विलक्षणः कश्चिद्विचारः सोयमीदृशः ॥१३॥

13. (*a*) I certainly cannot be this body—a mere collection of the various *Tatvas*; nor can I be any one of the senses (for the same reason), I must certainly be something quite apart from both of them :—This is &c.

अज्ञानप्रभवं सर्वं ज्ञानेन प्रविलीयते ।
संकल्पो विविधः कर्त्ता विचारः सोयमीदृशः ॥१४॥

14. (*b*) Everything emanates from ignorance, and melts away into knowledge; (*c*) the various fancies the *antaskarana* must be the (as understood by us) creator—This is &c.

एतयोर्यदुपादानमेकं सूक्ष्मं सदव्ययम् ।
यथैवमृद्घटादीनां विचारः सोयमी दृशः॥१५॥

15. (*d*) The material cause of these two, ignorance and fancy, is the incomprehensibly minute but unique and undecaying everlasting *sat*, just as the earth is the cause of jars etc—This &c.

अहमेकोऽपिसूक्ष्मश्च ज्ञाता साक्षी सदव्ययः ।
तदहं नात्र संदेहो विचारः सोयमीदृशः ॥१६॥

16. There is no doubt that *I* am one with that supreme *ego*, I am the very ego, which is common to all men, which is unique and one, which is incomprehensibly small, the subject of all perception, the everpresent witness, (seeing everything without the ordinary means of knowledge), the ever existent undecaying, spirit :—This &c.

आत्मा विनिष्कलो ह्येको देहो बहुभिरावृतः ।
तयोरैक्यं प्रपश्यंति किमज्ञानमतःपरम् ॥१७॥

17. The one *Atman*, the ever present Universal spirit—is free from all conditions (as organs of sense &c.), whereas the *Deha* i. e. *lingadeha* or astral body is bound by many :* what ignorance could surpass that of those who confound these two together ?

आत्मा नियामकश्चांतर्देहो बाह्यो नियम्यकः ।
तयोरैक्यं० ॥१८॥

18. The *Átman* is the internal governor of this *deha* which is the governed and therefore external : what ignorance &c.

आत्मा ज्ञानमयः पुण्यो देहो मांसमयोऽशुचिः
तयोरैक्यं० ॥१९॥

19. Tho *Atman* is all conscious Intelligence and all holiness : the deha i. e. the *Sthúladeha* or physical body is all flesh and blood, (i. e. inert) and therefore unclean : what ignorance &c.

---

* i. e. 17. The 5 *Prans* +5 *Dnyanendriya* +5 *Karmendriyas* + Buddhi + Ahankara = 17.

आत्मा प्रकाशकः स्वच्छो देहस्तामसउच्यते ।
तयोरैक्यं० ॥२०॥

20. The *Atman* is the illumination of the Universe and purity itself; the *deha* is all darkness (evolved from ignorance) what ignorance &c.

आत्मा नित्यो हिसद्रूपो देहोऽनित्यो ह्यसन्मयः ।
तयोरैक्यं० ॥२१॥

21. The *Atman* is permanent, eternal and therefore existence itself: whereas the *dehas* are non-eternal (subject to change) and non-existence incarnate : what ignorance &c.

आत्मनस्तत्प्रकाशत्वं यत्पदार्थाऽवभासनं ।
नाग्न्यादिदीप्तिवद्दीप्तिर्भवत्यांध्यं यतोनिशि ॥२२॥

22. That is the self-illuminating power of *Atman*, which enlightens *all* the objects of this Universe : it is not any ordinary light like that of fire or any other thing, which has no power to interfere with the presence of darkness in any the same contiguous place.*

देहोहमित्ययं मूढो धृत्वा तिष्ठत्यहोजनः ।
ममायमित्यपिज्ञात्वा घटद्दष्टेव सर्वदा ॥२३॥

23. It is very strange that people though always talking of this *deha* as something belonging to *me* (the subjective Atman) and therefore apart from He who possesses it, like one seeing a jar of earth talking of it as seen by him, and therefore, apart from him, should rest contented with identifying this *ego* with its (temporary tenement) *deha*?

---

* It may be argued that if the light of the Atman is unlike that of fire etc. for reason of the latter being impotent to dispel all darkness, where did any one observe the absence of darkness, for the light of the universal Atman being present everywhere? The Vedantin, will retort, it is only on account of the illumination proceeding from the Atman that darkness or fire or any such thing becomes comprehensible. It is that self-sustaining light which illumines all and is not opposed in its nature to any thing.

ब्रह्मैवाहं समः शांतः सच्चिदानंदलक्षणः ।
नाहं देहो ह्यसद्रूपो ज्ञानमित्युच्यते बुधैः ॥२४॥

24. The *ego* i. e. the substratum of the ego—the (subjective *atman*) is the Universal *Atman, Brahma,* being, with it, unique and one, ever-existent and self-illumined, free from all conditions, and by nature all existence, conscious intelligence and joy. The *deha* surely can never be the substratum of this ego: the deha which, is non-existence itself. This is called real knowledge by the wise (who have realised the real *Atmatatva.*)

निर्विकारो निराकारो निरवद्योहमव्ययः ।
नाहं देहो ह्यसद्रूपो ज्ञानमित्युच्यते बुधैः ॥२५॥

25. The *ego* is free from all change, without any form, undescribable and undecaying or indestructible. The *Deha* &c.

निरामयो निराभासो निर्विकल्पोहमाततः।
नाहंदेहो० ॥२६॥

26. The ego is beyond all disease, not within the reach of comprehension, free from all imagination, and all—pervading. The Deha &c.

निर्गुणो निष्क्रियो नित्यो नित्यमुक्तोहमच्युतः ।
नाहंदेहो० ॥२७॥

27. It is unaffected by the three *Gunas*—qualities—of matter,—*Sattva, Rajas* and *Tamas*—motionless, eternal, ever free from all conditions, undecaying and unique. The *deha* &c.

निर्मलो निश्चलोनंतः शुद्धोहमजरोमरः ।
नाहंदेहो० ॥२८॥

28. It is, again, free from every impurity—ignorance caused by *Avidyá*—Immoveable, Infinite, Holy, Immortal, and Unborn. The *deha* &c.

स्वदेहे शोभनं संतं पुरुषाख्यं च संमतम् ।
किं मूर्ख शून्यमात्मानं देहातीतं करोषि भोः ॥२९॥

29. Oh you Ignorant fool! when you have got in your own body the holy *Atman*, which is evidently different from the body, and which is known as the *Purusha* (residing in the body of men, in the form of the *ego*), how can you (in spite of this testimony) assert that this Atman is *nothing*, is mere void,—mere nil?

स्वात्मानं श्रुणु मूर्ख त्वं श्रुत्या युक्त्या च पूरुषम् ।
दहातितं सदाकारं सुदुर्दर्शं भवादृशैः ॥३०॥

30. (If abandoning your hypothesis as incompatible with the phenomena even of your own consciousness and existence, you should assert that there may be something, which however cannot be any thing other than the body itself). Oh ignorant one! know the ego within you to be that *Purusha* which is implied in the *S'rutis*, and demonstrated by Reasoning. It is other than the body in as much as it is the only one of whom you can predicate existence in the real sense of the word : but it is very difficult to be realised as such by people of your cast of mind.

अहं शब्देन विख्यात एकएव स्थितः परः।
स्थूलस्त्वनेकतां प्राप्तः कथंस्याद्देहकः पुमान् ॥३१॥

31. The *Atman*, which is the substratum of the *ego* in man, is one : and therefore different from the physical bodies which on the other hand are many. How can this body then be the *Atman*?

अहं द्रष्टृतया सिद्धो देहो दृश्यतया स्थितः ।
ममायमिति निर्द्देशात्कथं० ॥३२॥

32. The ego is well-established as the subject of all perception, whereas the body is the object : this is proved from the fact of our every time saying of the physical body as being "mine" "belonging to me" &c. How can this body &c.

अहं विकारहीनस्तु देहो नित्यं विकारवान् ।
इति प्रतीयते साक्षात्कथं० ॥ ३३ ॥

33. It is well-known to us in our daily experience that the *ego* is free from all change (caused by happiness, misery or time. The *ego remains the same* in childhood, young age, old age, though the body changes) whereas the physical body is subject to many. How can &c.

यस्मात्परमिति श्रुत्या तया पुरुषलक्षणम् ।
विनिर्णीतं विमूढेन कथं० ॥ ३४ ॥

34. The characteristics, Oh lord of the ignorant! of this Atman are laid down in the *S'ruti* यस्मात्परम् &c. (that is the *Purusha* than whom there is nothing higher &c.) How can &c.

सर्वं पुरुष एवेति सूक्ते पुरुषसंज्ञि ते ।
अप्युच्यते यतः श्रुत्या कथं० ॥ ३५ ॥

35. Again the *S'ruti* in the Purusha Sukta (the hymn to *Purusha* says, all this is *Purusha* etc. How then can &c.

असंगः पुरुषः प्रोक्तो बृहदारण्यकेऽपि च ।
अनंतमलसंश्लिष्टः कथं० ॥ ३६ ॥

36. Even in the Brihadáranyaka it is said "this *Purusha* is free from every thing etc"; How could this body besmeared with endless dirt be this *Purusha*?

तत्रैव च समाख्यातः स्वयं ज्योतिर्हि पूरुषः ।
जडः परप्रकाश्योसौ कथं० ॥ ३७ ॥

37. In the same *S'ruti*, it is said the *Purusha* is self-illumined &c. How could this body which is all darkness and illumined by something quite extraneous, be this *Purusha*?

प्रोक्तोऽपिकर्मकाण्डेन ह्यात्मादेहाद्विलक्षणः ।
नित्यश्च तत्फलं भुङ्क्ते देहपातादनंतरम् ॥ ३७ ॥

38. Even that part of the Vedas, which inculcates the performance of various religious ceremonies (as contra-distinguished from that part which inculcates the usefulness of knowledge only) describes the *Átman* as different from the *deha*; and as one, eternal, and therefore subsisting to undergo, after the destruction of its material coil, the results of actions done during any previous life.

लिङ्गं चानेकसंयुक्तं चलं दृश्यं विकारि च ।
अव्यापकमसद्रूपं तत्कथंस्यात्पुमानयम् ॥ ३९ ॥

39. Even the *astral body* is made up of many things (not one), is unstable, is the object of perception, is subject to change, limited, and non-existent. How could this astral body ever be the *Purusha*?

एवं देहद्वयादन्य आत्मा पुरुष ईश्वरः ।
सर्वात्मा सर्वरूपश्च सर्वातीतोहमव्ययः ॥ ४० ॥

40. Thus the *Átman* is evidently different from these two bodies, and is the Purusha, the Lord, the Soul of All, every thing in itself, free from all conditions, present in every one as the substratum of the ego, and indestructible.

इत्यात्मदेहभागेन प्रपञ्चस्यैव सत्यता ।
यथोक्ता तर्कशास्त्रेण ततः किंपुरुषार्थता ॥ ४१ ॥

41. Thus the enunciation of the difference between the two bodies and the *Átman* involving an (indirect) assertion of the reality of the material transitional Universe, given in a manner after the principles of the *Tarkas'ástra* (Nyaya), compasses but a very insignificant aim in life.*

---

* For it leaves the state of final absolution open to some objections as to its utility or quality, based on the *duality* of the cosmic principle.

इत्यात्मदेहभेदेन देहात्मत्वं निवारितम् ।
इदानीं देहभेदस्य ह्यसत्त्वं स्फुटमुच्यते ॥ ४२ ॥

42. The object however of this enunciation of the vital fundamental difference between the two bodies and the Átman is (not to establish the reality of the material universe but) to dissipate the ignorance of confounding or identifying the Átman with the *dehas*. It yet remains, however, to clearly demonstrate the unreality of the difference between the two, i. e. it remains clearly to establish that the *dehas* have no existence independent of, and without the *Átman*.

चैतन्यस्यैकरूपत्वाद्भेदो युक्तो न कर्हिचित् ।
जीवत्वं च मृषा ज्ञेयं रज्जौ सर्पग्रहो यथा ॥ ४३ ॥

43. As *Chaitanya* or absolute consciousness is but uniform and unique, it cannot admit of a second, it cannot admit of a division. Even the individual soul must then be accepted to be futile, like the delusion of snake in a rope.

रज्ज्वज्ञानात् क्षणेनैव यद्वद्रज्जुर्हि सर्पिणी ।
भाति तद्वच्चितिः साक्षाद्विश्वाकारेण केवला ॥ ४४ ॥

44. As through ignorance the rope, appears for the time, to be a snake, so does the unconditioned consciousness—*chit*—, (*Brahma*)—appear in the form of this so-called material universe.

उपादानं प्रपंचस्य ब्रह्मणोऽन्यन्नविद्यते ।
तस्मात्सर्वप्रपञ्चोयं ब्रह्मैवास्ति न चेतरत् ॥४५॥

45. The material cause of this transitional universe can be nothing else than *Brahma*; it follows therefore that the whole universe is Brahma itself and nothing else.

व्याप्यव्यापकता मिथ्या सर्वमात्मेति शासनात् ।
इति ज्ञाते परे तत्वे भेदस्यावसरः कुतः ॥ ४६ ॥

46. In as much as it is ordained that "All is *Átman*," the distinction between the pervading and the pervaded or subject and object, is illusory. This, the highest truth being realised, there could be little room for the distinction of subject and object etc.

श्रुत्या निवारितं नूनं नानात्वं स्वमुखेन हि ।
कथं भासो भवेदन्यः स्थिते चाद्वयकारणे ॥ ४७ ॥

47. When the *S'ruti* has by denouncing in loud terms the existence of any variety in this (Brahma), fused all the material, instrumental and final causes into one unique consciousness, how could there be even the least shadow of any other thing? (as the pervading and pervaded, subject and object etc.)

दोषोपि विहितः श्रुत्या मृत्योर्मृत्युं स गच्छति ।
इह पश्यति नानात्वं मायया वञ्चितो नरः ॥४८॥

48. The *S'ruti* has not rested here, but has fastened an awful sin to the belief in the existence of the cause as separate from the effect, in the words "He who led away by *Máyá* or illusion, accepts any variety in this (Absolute *Átman*) passes from death to death (i. e. is born and reborn often and often, and does not attain to final beatitude.)"

ब्रह्मणः सर्वभूतानि जायन्तेपरमात्मनः ।
तस्मादेतानिब्रह्मैव भवन्तीत्यवधारयेत् ॥ ४९ ॥

49. In as much as the universe exists in the Absolute *Átman*, all-embracing Brahma, it must be understood to be one, with Brahma, its original cause.

ब्रह्मैव सर्वनामानि रूपाणि विविधानि च ।
कर्माण्यपि समग्राणि बिभर्तीति श्रुतिर्जगौ ॥५०॥

50. Moreover the *S'ruti* plainly declares that all kinds of names, forms, and actions are sustained in, and through *Brahma*.

सुवर्णाज्जायमानस्य सुवर्णत्वं च शाश्वतम् ।
ब्रह्मणो जायमानस्य ब्रह्मत्वं च तथाभवेत् ॥५१॥

51. As the being golden of that which is made of gold is eternal and unchanging, so should be the being *Brahma* of that which proceeds from Brahma.

स्वल्पमप्यन्तरं कृत्वा जीवात्मपरमात्मनोः ।
यः संतिष्ठाति मूढात्मा भयं तस्याभिभाषितम् ॥५२॥

52. The opinions of that ignorant man, who abides by even the faintest distinction between *Jiva* and *Paramátman*, are very dangerous and pernicious.

यत्राज्ञानाद्भवेद्द्वैतमितरस्तत्र पश्यति ।
आत्मत्वेन यदा सर्वं नेतरस्तत्र चाण्वपि ॥ ५३॥

53. Distinctions crop up only so long as *duality* is maintained through ignorance, but when the whole is seen as in and of *Átman*, there could not exist the least shadow of distinction.

यस्मिन् सर्वाणि भूतानि ह्यात्मत्वेन विजानतः ।
न वै तस्य भवेन्मोहो न च शोकोऽद्वितीयतः ॥ ५४॥

54. In the condition in which the enlightened identify the whole with *Átman*, there enters not the faintest tinge of delusion, or sorrow, in consequence of the cause of such delusion or sorrow being destroyed with the dissipation of the idea of duality.

अयमात्मा हि ब्रह्मैव सर्वात्मकतया स्थितः ।
इति निर्द्धारितंश्रुत्या बृहदारण्यसंस्थया ॥ ५५ ॥

55. The S'ruti in the Brahadáranyaka has declared that this soul is Brahma, and stands as the soul and substance of the universe.

अनुभूतोऽप्ययं लोको व्यवहारक्षमोऽपि सन् ।
असद्रूपो यथास्वप्न उत्तरक्षणबाधतः ॥ ५६ ॥

56. The universe though it be the subject of daily experience, and though it be the object of our constant intercourse (and therefore the living cause of constant delusion, so on &c. vide 54) is unreal like a dream in as much as its *existence* even in the moment next its birth is not provable.

स्वप्नो जागरणेऽलीकः स्वप्नेऽपि जागरो नहि ।
द्वयमेव लये नास्ति लयोपि ह्युभयोर्न च ॥५७॥

57. For example: dreams are unreal during waking; nor is the waking condition possible in dreams. Both however are not to be found in deep absorption, as in dreamless sleep, which again is not experienced in either.

त्रयमेवं भवेन्मिथ्या गुणत्रयविनिर्मितम् ।
अस्य द्रष्टा गुणातीतो नित्यो ह्येक श्चिदात्मकः॥५८॥

58. Thus, all these three conditions are unreal, being the illusive creations of *máyá* with its three *gunas*; the real, permanent, and unique one is the spirit, which stands aloof from these three *gunas* as the witness of all these conditions.

यद्वन्मृदि घटभ्रान्तिं शुक्तौ वा रजतस्थितिम् ।
तद्वद्ब्रह्मणि जीवत्वं वीक्ष्यमाणे न पश्यति ॥ ५९ ॥

59. Just as after mature contemplation one does not find a jar in the clay of which it is made, or silver in a lump of nacre, so will the enlightened, on deep meditation, be free from the delusion of believing *Jiva* to be separate from *Brahma*.

यथा मृदि घटो नाम कनके कुण्डलाभिधा ।
शुक्तौ हि रजतख्यातिर्जीवशब्दस्तथापरे ॥६०॥

60. The jar exists in earth, the ring in gold, and silver, in nacre—but all in *mere name*, so does *Jiva* exist in Brahma.

यथैव व्योम्नि नीलत्वं यथा नीरं मरुस्थले ।
पुरुषत्वं यथा स्थाणौ तद्वद्विश्वं चिदात्मनि ॥६१॥

61. Just as blueness appears in the sky, or water in the mirage, or as a man is seen in a post, so does the universe appear in the *Atman.*

यथैव शून्ये वैतालो गन्धर्वाणीं पुरं यथा ।
यथाकाशे द्विचंद्रत्वं तद्वत्सत्ये जगत्स्थितिः ॥६२॥

62. Just as one sees a giant in vacancy; a castle in the air or two moons instead of one in the sky, so do ignorant persons see the universe as apart from Brahma.

यथा तरंगकल्लोलैर्जलमेव स्फुरत्यलम् ।
पात्ररूपेण ताम्रं हि ब्रह्माण्डौघैस्तथात्मता ॥६३॥

63. Just as all that appear is water whether in the form of waves or ripples on the surface, or as all again that appears is copper whether as pots or anything, so are all the various forms in the universe but mere manifestations of the *Atman.*

घटनाम्ना यथा पृथ्वी पटनाम्ना हि तन्तवः ।
जगन्नाम्ना चिदाभाति ज्ञेयं तत्तदभावतः ॥६४॥

64. Just as it is earth alone that appears under the *name* of a jar, or just as they are the threads only that appear under the *name* of a cloth, so does the Illumined—spirit—go under the *name* of the universe; this spirit can be grasped by the negation of the various imaginary adjuncts superinduced, as *name, form &c.*

सर्वोऽपि व्यवहारस्तु ब्रह्मणाक्रिय तेजनैः ।
अज्ञानान्न विजानन्ति मृदेवाहि घटादिकम् ॥६५॥

65. All intercourse proceeds of, and through *Brahma.* It is through ignorance only that people do not clearly understand that all the jars and pots that appear are but earth and earth alone.

कार्यकारणता नित्समास्ते घटमृदोर्यथा ।
तथैव श्रुतियुक्तिभ्यां प्रपञ्चब्रम्हणोरिह ॥६६॥

66. Just as the relation of cause and effect between clay and a jar, is constant, so in the question at issue is that of Brahma and the unreal universe; this is loudly declared by Revelation and clearly verified by reason.

गृह्यमाणे घटे यद्वन्मृत्तिका याति वै बलात् ।
वीक्ष्यमाणे प्रपञ्चेपि ब्रम्हैवाभाति भासुरम् ॥६७॥

67. Just as the consciousness of clay is forced upon our mind, when we are contemplating of a jar only, so even though dealing with the unreal universe, we are through it and in it, rendered forcibly and as it were intuitively conscious of the all pervading Brahma.

सदैवात्मा विशुद्धोस्ति ह्यशुद्धोभाति वै सदा ।
यथैव द्विविधा रज्जुर्ज्ञानिनोऽज्ञानिनोऽनिशम् ॥६८॥

68. The *Atman* though ever pure, ever appears impure just as the same cord appears as a serpent and as a cord to an ignorant and a knowing man respectively.

यथैव मृण्मयःकुंभस्तद्वद्देहोपि चिन्मयः ।
आत्मानात्मविभागोयं मुधैव क्रियते बुधैः ॥६९॥

69. Just as the jar is all earth, so this body is all spirit; the divison of *Atman* and *not Atman* is made by the ignorant for no purpose whatever.

सर्पत्वेन यथारज्जू रजतत्वेनशुक्तिका ।
विनिर्णीता विमूढेन देहत्वेन तथात्मता ॥७०॥

70. Just as a cord is understood to be a snake, or a lump of nacre to be a lump of silver, so do the ignorant determine the physical body to be the *Atman*.

घटत्वेन यथा पृथ्वी पटत्वेनैव तन्तवः ।
विनिर्णीता विमूढेन देहत्वेन तथाऽऽत्मता ॥ ७१ ॥

71. Just as clay is confounded with the jar made of it, or the threads with the cloth, so do &c.

कनकं कुण्डलत्वेन तरंगत्वेन वै जलम् ।
विनिर्णीता० ॥ ७२ ॥

72. Just as gold is confounded with the rings made of it or water with the waves surging over it, so &c.

पुरुषत्वे यथा स्थाणुर्जलत्वेन मरीचिका ।
विनिर्णीता० ॥ ७३ ॥

73. Just as a post is taken for a man or the mirage for real water, so do &c.

गृहत्वेनैव काष्ठानि खड्गत्वेनैव लोहता ।
विनिर्णीता० ॥ ७४ ॥

74. Just as the materials are confounded with the house, or the iron with the sword made of it, so do &c.

यथा वृक्षविपर्यासो जलाद्भवति कस्यचित् ।
तद्वदात्मनि देहत्वं पश्यत्यज्ञानयोगतः ॥ ७५ ॥

75. Just as one seeing at a tree through water sees it inverted, so does the material body appear as *Átman* to one viewing it through ignorance.

पोतेन गच्छतः पुंसः सर्वं भातीव चञ्चलम् ।
तद्वदा० ॥ ७६ ॥

76. Just as to one sailing in a boat every thing appears to be in motion, so &c.

पीतत्वं हि यथा शुभ्रे दोषाद्भवति कस्यचित् ।
तद्वदा० ॥ ७७ ॥

77. Just as a "jaundiced eye sees every thing yellow," so &c.

चक्षुर्भ्यां भ्रमशीलाभ्यां सर्वं भाति भ्रमात्मकम् ।
तद्व० ॥ ७८ ॥

78. With eyes which are as it were by nature in delusion, every thing appears illusion, so &c.

अलातं भ्रमणेनैव वर्त्तुलं भाति सूर्यवत् ।
तद्वदा० ॥ ७९ ॥

79. Just as the circle made by a fire-brand, appears like the disc of the sun, so &c.

महत्त्वे सर्ववस्तूनामणुत्वं ह्यतिदूरतः ।
तद्वदा० ॥ ८० ॥

80. Just as things which are prodigiously large appear small in consequence of distance, so &c.

सूक्ष्मत्वे सर्वभावानां स्थूलत्वं चोपनेत्रतः ।
तद्वदा० ॥ ८१ ॥

81. Just as the smallest objects appear very large when viewed through powerful spectacles, so &c.

काचभूमौ जलत्वं वा जलभूमौ हि काचता ।
तद्वदा० ॥ ८२ ॥

82. As a floor of glass should be imagined to be filled with water or vice versa, so &c.

यद्वदग्नौ मणित्वं हि मणौ वा वह्निता पुमान् ।
तद्वदा० ॥ ८३ ॥

83. As one should confound fire with a jewel or vice versa so &c.

अभ्रेषु सत्सु धावत्सु सोमो धावति भाति वै ।
तद्वदा० ॥ ८४ ॥

84. As the moon appears to be in motion through the clouds which really are moving, so &c.

यथैव दिग्विपर्यासो मोहाद्भवति कस्यचित् ।
तद्वदा० ॥ ८५ ॥

85. As some one through confusion loses all distinction between the different points of the compass, so &c.

यथा शशी जले भाति चञ्चलत्वेन कस्यचित् ।
तद्वदा० ॥ ८६ ॥

86. Just as the moon, (on account of its reflection) appears moving under the surface of water to some one, so &c.

एवमात्मन्यविद्यातो देहाध्यासो हि जायते ।
स एवात्मपरिज्ञानाल्लीयते च परात्मनि ॥ ८७ ॥

87. In this manner then, arises the delusion of *matter* (*deha*) in the (spiritual) *Átman*, which (delusion) melts away in the proper realisation of Brahma, by the help of right knowledge.

सर्वमात्मतया ज्ञातं जगत्स्थावरजङ्गमम् ।
अभावात्सर्वभावानां देहस्य चात्मता कुतः ॥ ८८ ॥

88. When the whole universe, movable as well as immovable, is known to be Átman by the negation of all substance which appear to exist apart from it, there hardly remains any room even to say that this material body is *Átman*.

आत्मानं सततं जानन्कालं नय महाद्युते ।
प्रारब्धमखिलं भुञ्जन्नोद्वेगं कर्तुमर्हसि ॥ ८९ ॥

89. Oh enlightened one! spend all your time in ever contemplating upon the *Átman*, consuming out, without repining or pain, the fruits of your *Prárabdha*.

उत्पन्नेप्यात्मविज्ञाने प्रारब्धं नैव मुञ्चति ।
इति यच्छ्रूयते शास्त्रे तन्निराक्रियतेऽधुना ॥ ९० ॥

90. We now proceed to explain the opinion often declared by the *Sástras* that no body is free from the operations of the law of *Prárabdha*, even though he should have acquired full knowledge of the *Átman*.

तत्त्वज्ञानोदयादूर्ध्वं प्रारब्धं नैव विद्यते ।
देहादीनामसत्त्वात्तु यथा स्वप्नो विबोधतः ॥ ९१ ॥

91. After the knowledge of the *real* has arisen, there remains no room for *Prárabdha,* in as much as this material body &c. (the plane on which the effects of *Prárabdha,* manifest themselves) are then reduced as it were to nothing : just as there is no room for dream after waking.

कर्म जन्मान्तरीयं यत्प्रारब्धमिति कीर्तितम् ।
तत्तु जन्मांतराभावात्पुंसो नैवास्ति कर्हिचित् ॥ ९२ ॥

92. That *Karma* acquired in a previous birth which is called *Prárabdha* (with respect to the present life), has no existence (in the form of *Sanchita* for a future birth) in as much as the man has no other birth to go through.

स्वप्नदेहो यथाध्यस्तस्तथैवायं हि देहकः ।
अध्यस्तस्य कुतो जन्म जन्माभावे हि तत्कुतः ॥ ९३ ॥

93. Just as the body at work during dream is a mere illusion, so also is this our physical body. How, then, could an illusion, be said to take birth, and when it does not take birth how again could it be said to exist?

उपादानं प्रपञ्चस्य मृद्भाण्डस्येव कथ्यते ।
अज्ञानं चैव वेदान्तैस्तस्मिन्नष्टे क्व विश्वता ॥ ९४ ॥

94. The *Vedantas* declare *ignorance* (and *Brahma*) to be the material cause of the universe, just as earth of a jar &c. When this ignorance is destroyed where could the universe subsist?

यथा रज्जुं परित्यज्य सर्पं गृह्णाति वै भ्रमात् ।
तद्वत्सत्यमविज्ञाय जगत्पश्यति मूढधीः ॥ ९५ ॥

95. Just as some one should out of confusion understand a rope to be a serpent, so an ignorant man leaving aside the truth sets up this (material) transitory universe in its place.

रज्जुरूपे परिज्ञाते सर्पखण्डं न तिष्ठति ।
अधिष्ठाने तथा ज्ञाते प्रपञ्चः शून्यतां गतः ॥ ९६ ॥

96. The cord being fully known the serpent disappears at once : so the great substance and support of the universe being known, the universe reduces itself to nothing.

देहस्याऽपि प्रपञ्चत्वात्प्रारब्धावस्थितिः कुतः ।
अज्ञानिजनबोधार्थं प्रारब्धं वक्ति वै श्रुतिः ॥ ९७ ॥

97. As this physical body is thus a mere illusion where could there be any room for the play of *Prárabdha*. Hence the *Prárabdha* &c. described in the *Srutis* are for the enlightenment of the ignorant only.

[illegible]
बहुत्वं तन्निषेधार्थं श्रुत्या गीतं च यत्स्फुटम् ॥ ९८ ॥

98. The *Plural* used in the *S'ruti* "the highest good of all being reached, all his *Karmas* are destroyed &c." is to negative distinctly the possibility of the action of *Prárabdha* (as well as the other two ; *Sanchita* and *Kriyamáṇa*).

उच्यतेऽज्ञैर्बलाच्चैतत्तदानर्थद्वयागमः ।
वेदान्तमतहानं च यतो ज्ञानमिति श्रुतिः ॥ ९९ ॥

99. If the ignorant should still maintain the possibility of *Prárabdha* and its action, they will over and above involving themselves in two glaring absurdities, (1. impossibility of *moksha* on account of there being a second—a *Prárabdha* —Superior even to *Brahma* : 2. *moksha* being thus, rendered impossible the utility of the *Dnyánmárga*—the way of knowledge—will be nullified), run counter to the teachings of the *Vedánta*. It therefore follows that we must go by the said *Sruti* (Vide Stanza 98) which directs the way to real knowledge.

त्रिपञ्चाङ्गान्यथो वक्ष्ये पूर्वोक्तस्य हि लब्धये ।
तैश्च सर्वैः सदा कार्यं निदिध्यासनमेव तु ॥ १०० ॥

100. Hence forward (for the instruction of those who require to be taken step by step to the realisation of the said truth) we begin to propound the 15 stages necessary for the acquisition of the knowledge described before. Knowing all these one must use all of them towards acquiring a habit of constant, firm and active meditation.

नित्याभ्यासादृते प्राप्तिर्न भवेत्सच्चिदात्मनः ।
तस्माद्ब्रह्म निदिध्यासेज्जिज्ञासुः श्रेयसे चिरम् ॥ १०१ ॥

101. The ever—existent, and all—conscious *A'tman* is not realised without a constant and rigid practice (of the rules to be described); therefore one desirous of obtaining absolution must ever meditate upon *Brahma.*

यमो हि नियमस्त्यागो मौनं देशश्च कालता ।
आसनं मूलबन्धश्च देहसाम्यं च दृक्स्थितिः ॥ १०२ ॥
प्राणसंयमनं चैव प्रत्याहारश्च धारणा ।
आत्मध्यानं समाधिश्च प्रोक्तान्यंगानि वै क्रमात् ॥१०३॥

102.–103. The fifteen stages in order are : 1 *Yama*, 2 *Niyama*, 3 *Tyága*, 4 *Mauna*, 5 *Desh*, 6 *Kála*, 7 *Asana*, 8 *Mùlabandha*, 9 *Dehasàmya*, 10 *Driksthiti*, 11 *Pránasamyamana*, 12 *Pratyáhára*, 13 *Dhárana*, 14 *Atmadhyana*, 15 *Samadhi*.

सर्वं ब्रह्मेति विज्ञानादिन्द्रियग्रामसंयमः ।
यमोऽयमिति संप्रोक्तोऽभ्यसनीयो मुहुर्मुहुः ॥ १०४ ॥

104. The natural restraint over all the senses arising from, the conviction of *everything* being *Brahma*, is the real *yama*, and it should be repeatedly studied.*

---

* अहिंसा, सत्यं, अस्तेयं, ब्रह्मचर्यं, क्षमा, धृतिः । दया, आर्जवं मिताहारः शौचं चैव यमा दश ॥ १६–१–॥ हठप्रदीपिका ॥ The *yama* of *Hatha* or physical, *yoga*, comprises ten formulas of conduct all however tending to secure the mental condition described in 104. The same remark holds good for all other illustrations to be cited from works on *Hatha yoga*.

सजातयिप्रवाहश्च विजातीयतिरस्कृतिः ।
नियमो हि परानन्दो नियमात्क्रियते बुधैः ॥ १०५ ॥

105. The union with the homogeneous (i. e., constant and invariably inseparable consciousness of unity with Brahma), and separation from the heterogeneous (such notions as of the universe and Brahma being apart from each other &c.), is the *Niyama* described in the *Srutis;—niyama* the highest happiness; such are thought of by the wise.*

त्यागः प्रपञ्चरूपस्य चिदात्मत्वावलोकनात् ।
त्यागो हि महतां पूज्यः सद्यो मोक्षमयो यतः ॥ १०६ ॥

106. The abandonment of this illusion (of form and name) by the recognition of the non-material, ever enlightened Brahma everywhere, is the *Tyága* honoured by the great, as leading to immediate absolution.†

यस्माद्वाचो निवर्तन्तेऽप्राप्य मनसा सह ।
यन्मौनं योगिभिर्गम्यं तद्भवेत्सर्वदा बुधः ॥ १०७ ॥

107. The enlightened must ever try to possess that *Mauna*—that indescribable Brahma—which, though the mind turns back baffled from it, and though words cannot describe it, is ever to be found in those who are devoted to the path of pure knowledge.‡

---

* तपः, संतोष, आस्तिक्यं, दानं, ईश्वर पूजनं,। सिद्धांतवाक्यश्रवणं, न्हीमति, श्च तपो, हुतम् ॥ नियमा दश संप्रोक्ता योगशास्त्रविशारदैः ॥ idem.

† This *Tyâga* must it seems be understood as opposed to the *Tyaga* or abandonment of one's duties and *Karmas* in life—as understood by superficial *Vedantins*.

‡ This *maunâ* is opposed to the ordinary practice of restraining the tongue &c.

वाचो यस्मान्निवर्तन्ते तद्वक्तुं केन शक्यते ।
प्रपञ्चो यदि वक्तव्यः सोऽपि शब्दविवर्जितः ॥ १०८ ॥
इति वा तद्भवेन्मौनं सतां सहजसंज्ञितम् ।
गिरा मौनं तु बालानां प्रयुक्तं ब्रह्मवादिभिः ॥ १०९ ॥

108.–109. Who can describe that (Brahma) which words are not able to comprehend? If this universe of illusion even were subjected to examination, that also is beyond the reach of speech. Hence this may be the real *Mauna* (viz. abandonment of all doubts as to the relation of *Brahma* and *Jagat*) known to the wise as *Sahaja Sthiti*—Native condition;—where as the *Mauna* ordinarily known in the form of restraining the tongue is pronounced by the Advaiti, to be simply childish.

आदावन्ते च मध्ये च जनो यस्मिन्न विद्यते ।
येनेदं सततं व्याप्तं स देशो विजनः स्मृतः ॥ ११० ॥

110. That is the real "solitary, *Des'a*" (place) wherein the universe does not exist in the beginning, middle, or end; and which is to be found through the whole of this (material life).*

कलनात्सर्वभूतानां ब्रह्मादीनां निमेषतः ।
कालशब्देन निर्दिष्टो ह्यखण्डानन्दअद्वयः ॥ १११ ॥

111. In consequence of its being support and sustenance of all actions, such as even the winking of the eye &c., of all up to *Brnhma* and others, the word *Kâla* indicates the real uninterrupted and unique fountain of joy. (*Brahma*).†

---

* सुराज्ये धार्मिके देशे सुभिक्षे निरुपद्रवे । धनुःप्रमाणपर्यंते शिलाग्निजलवर्जिते । एकांते मठिकामध्ये स्थातव्यं हठयोगिना ॥ हठ. प्र० ॥

† This kâla may by taken as opposed to the time observed in performing prânâyâma &c.

सुखेनैव भवेद्यास्मिन्नजस्रं ब्रह्मचिंतनम् ।
आसनं तद्विजानीयान्नेतरत्सुखनाशनम् ॥ ११२ ॥

112. That in which one can easily and uninterruptedly meditate upon *Brahma* is the most proper *Ásana,* and not any other interfering with one's ease and happiness.*

सिद्धं यत्सर्वभूतादि विश्वाधिष्ठानमव्ययम् ।
यस्मिन् सिद्धाः समाविष्टास्तद्वै सिद्धासनं विदुः ॥ ११३ ॥

113. That which is the eternal and well-known container of the universe of being, and that in which the *Siddhas* are ever sitting at ease, is the real *Siddhàsana.*†

यन्मूलं सर्वभूतानां यन्मूलं चित्तबन्धनम् ।
मूलबन्धः सदा सेव्यो योग्योऽसौ राजयोगिनाम् ॥११४॥

114. That which is the origin of all Being, and that on whom depends the original (ignorance) obstruction of the *manas,* is the *múlabandha* to be always practiced, and is the only one to be taken up by students of *Raja* or mental *yoga.*‡

अङ्गानां समतां विद्यात्समे ब्रह्मणि लीयते ।
नो चेन्नैव समानत्वमृजुत्वं शुष्कवृक्षवत् ॥ ११५ ॥

115. That is *Dehasámya* by which the physical body (naturally crooked and distorted) becomes on account of its being viewed as of Brahma, immersed in Brahma. If this is not accomplished, the forcible straightening of the limbs, like that of the dead trunk of a tree, is certainly the least of *Dehasámya.*

---

* As opposed to the 8 or any indefinite number of *Ásanas* as *Sidhás-an Padmàsana, Mayúrásan* &c.—all implying certain positions of the body accompanied by an amount of physical exertion and exercise.

† मेढ्रादुपरि विन्यस्य सव्यं गुल्फं तथोपरि । गुल्फांतरं च निक्षिप्य सिद्धासनमिदं भवेत् ॥ हठ. प्र०॥.

‡ पार्ष्णिभागेन संपीड्य योनीमाकुंचयेद् गुदम् । अपानमूर्ध्वमाकृष्य मूलबंधोऽभिधीयते ॥ हठ. प्र०॥.

दृष्टिं ज्ञानमयीं कृत्वा पश्येद्ब्रह्ममयं जगत् ।
सा दृष्टिः परमोदारा न नासाग्रावलोकिनी ॥ ११६ ॥

116. That one, having converted his internal eye into one of pure knowledge, should view the whole of this transitional universe as Brahma, is the real concentration of the eye *(Drik-sthiti)*; and not the one wherein the eye is fixed on the tip of one's nose.*

दृष्टिदर्शनदृश्यानां विरामो यत्र वा भवेत् ।
दृष्टिस्तत्रैव कर्त्तव्या न नासाग्रावलोकिनी ॥ ११७ ॥

117. Or, the fixing of the (internal) ego on that in which the triad of the seer, sight and seen is reduced to unity—is the real concentration &c.

चित्तादिसर्वभावेषु ब्रह्मत्वेनैव भावनात् ।
निरोधः सर्ववृत्तीनां प्राणायामः स उच्यते ॥११८॥

118. The constant and permanent obstruction of all the senses (internal), through the process of viewing upon all objects such as the mind and its creations &c. as in and of Brahma is called *Pránáyáma.*†

---

* Compare the various *Mudrâs* of *Hotha yoga.*

† चले वाते चलं चित्तं निश्चले निश्चलं भवेत् ।
योगी स्थाणुत्वमाप्नोति ततो वायुं निरोधयेत्

* * * * *

बद्ध पद्मासनो योगी प्राणं चंद्रेण पूरयेत् ।
धारयित्वा यथाशक्ति भूयः सूर्येण रेचयेत् ॥
प्राणं सूर्येण चाकृष्य पूरयेदुदरं शनैः ।
विधिवत् कुंभकं कृत्वा पुनश्चंद्रेण रेचयेत् ॥ हठ०प्र० ॥

निषेधनं प्रपञ्चस्य रेचकाख्यः समीरणः ।
ब्रह्मैवाऽस्मीति या वृत्तिः पूरको वायुरीरितः ॥११९॥
ततस्तद्वृत्तिनैश्चल्यं कुंभकः प्राणसंयमः ।
अयं चाऽपि प्रबुद्धानामज्ञानां घ्राणपीडनम् ॥१२०॥

119, 120. The negation (as by resolving into Brahma &c) of this phenomenal illusion, is the real *Rechaka* (blowing out of the breath retained in the lungs); and the conviction "I am Brahma" is the real *Púraka* (the drawing in of the breath); and then the immovable concentration on that very conviction is the real *kumbhaka* (the retention of the breath in the lungs for some time). This is the real course of *Pránáyáma** but to be followed by the enlightened, whereas, the ignorant will go on torturing their nose for nothing.

विषयेष्वात्मतां दृष्ट्वा मनसश्चितिमज्जनम् ।
प्रत्याहारः स विज्ञेयोऽभ्यसनीयो मुमुक्षुभिः ॥१२१॥

121. The absorption of the mind in the ever-enlightened *Brahma* by resolving all objects into *Átman*, should be known as *Pratyáhára*, and should be practised by those who are desirous of absolution.†

It will be observed that the difference in the practice here indicated constitutes the real point of difference between Hatha or physical and Raja or mental yoga. The point to be reached by either is the same—restraint over the mind and its creations, and attainment of the condition of eternal *Samadhi* or concentration or identification with this principle of the universe —but the ways leading to this end are different. The former holds that the mind will be naturally and easily controlled by shutting up all the avenues of its communication with the external world—viz. the breath &c. The latter holds and perhaps correctly holds—that the shortness or length of the breath, is but an indication of the State of the mind and that therefore instead of fruitlessly and unnaturally stifling this breath we had much better curb the cause of all this breath and everything viz. the giant मनस् or the mind.

* The order of the process indicated in the Hatha yoga is 1st *Puraka* then *Kumbhaka* and then *Rechaka.*

† स्वविषयासंप्रयोगेचित्तस्यस्वरूपानुकारइन्द्रियाणां प्रत्याहारः ॥ पात० यो० सू० ॥ २. ५४. ॥

यत्र यत्र-मनो याति ब्रह्मणस्तत्र दर्शनात् ।
मनसो धारणं चैव धारणा सा परा मता ॥१२२॥

122. The steadiness of the mind arising from the recognition of *Brahma*, wherever it travels or goes, is the real and great *Dhárañá.**

ब्रह्मैवास्मीति सद्वृत्या निरालम्वतया स्थितिः ।
ध्यानशब्देन विख्याता परमानन्ददायिनी ॥१२३॥

123. The independent (free from any other idea as of *matter*, &c.) existence consequent upon the full sense of Being; arising from the conviction "I am *Brahma*," is the condition conducive to the highest joy, and is described as *Dhyána.*†

निर्विकारतया वृत्या ब्रह्माकारतया पुनः ।
वत्तिविस्मरणं सम्यक् समाधिर्ज्ञानसंज्ञकः ॥१२४॥

124. The negation of all mental action, by the mind's being reduced to a state beyond all change, and by its being ever merged into Brahma is called conscious *Samádhi.*‡

इमं चाकृत्रिमानन्दं तावत्साधु समभ्यसेत् ।
वश्यो यावत्क्षणात्पुंसः प्रयुक्तः सन्भवेत्स्वयम् ॥१२५॥

125. This natural course of joy should be studied by the wise only so long as they acquire the power of, at the spur of the moment, collecting and concentrating themselves.

---

* देशबन्धश्चित्तस्यधारणा ॥ पात० यो० सू०॥ ३. २. ॥

† तत्रप्रत्यैयकतानताध्यानम् ॥ पा० यो० सू० ३. २. ॥

‡ Even in *Raj yoga* समाधि is sometimes concisely defined as समाधिः संविदुत्पात्त also as तदेवार्थमात्रनिर्भासं स्वरूपशून्यामिव समाधिः ॥ पा० यो०सू०॥ ३. ३. The Hatha yoga has यदा संक्षीयते प्राणे मानसं च प्रलीयते । तदासमरसत्वं चसमाधि रभिधीयते ॥ हठ० प्र० ॥

ततः साधनानिर्मुक्तः सिद्धो भवति योगिराट् ।
तत्स्वरूपं न चैतस्य विषयो मनसो गिराम् ॥१२६॥

126. Then he (the practitioner) being free from the necessity of going through the said and similar processes, becomes the best of all accomplished successful ascetics. The condition of such an ascetic cannot easily be described in words or conceived by the mind.

समाधौ क्रियमाणे तु विघ्नान्यायान्ति वै बलात् ।
अनुसंधानराहित्यमालस्यं भोगलालसम् ॥१२७॥
लयस्तमश्च विक्षेपो रसास्वादश्च शून्यता ।
एवं यद्विघ्नबाहुल्यं त्याज्यं ब्रह्मविदाशनैः ॥१२८॥

127. 128. Even while assiduously practising *Samádhi,* numerous difficulties crop up in the way: Such as being put off the point of concentration; idleness; desire of illusive enjoyments; sleep; paralysis of the intellect; being drawn off by temporary objects of the universe; egoistical immersion in transitory joy; and dullness or torpidity of the mind. One knowing Brahma should try to gradually evade all these one after another.*

भाववृत्त्या हि भावत्वं शून्यवृत्त्या हि शून्यता ।
ब्रह्मवृत्त्या हि पूर्णत्वं तथा पूर्णत्वमभ्यसेत् ॥१२९॥

129. If one concentrates his mind on some object, or even on void, he becomes entirely filled with that object or that void: so one who fixes his mind on *Brahma* becomes completely

---

* एवमस्याङ्गिनो निर्विकल्पस्य लयविक्षेपकषायरसास्वादलक्षणाश्चत्वारोविघ्नाः संभवंति । लयस्तावदखंडवस्त्वनवलंबनेन चित्तवृत्तेर्निद्रा। अखंडवस्त्वनवलंबनेन चित्तवृत्तेरन्यावलंबनं विक्षेपः । लयविक्षेपाभावेऽपिचित्तवृत्तेरागादिवसानयस्तब्धीभावादखंडवस्त्वनवलंबनंकषायः । अखंडवस्त्वनवलंबेननाऽपिचित्तवृत्तेः सविकल्पकानंदास्वादनं रसास्वादः। समाध्यारंभसमये सविकल्पकानंदास्वादनं वा । अनेन विघ्नचतुष्टयेन विरहितं चित्तं निवातदीपवदचलं सदखंडचैतन्यमात्रमवतिष्ठते यदा तदा निर्विकल्पकसमाधिरुच्यते ॥ वेदान्तसार ॥

full of *Brahma*, sees *Brahma* everywhere. One should therefore study to become perfect i. e. full of *Brahma*.

ये हि वृत्तिं जहत्येनां ब्रह्माख्यां पावनीं पराम् ।
ते तु वृथैव जीवन्ति पशुभिश्च समा नराः ॥१३०॥

130. Those persons who abandon this holy and sublime mental attitude of *Brahma*, live to no purpose, and are though men equal to brutes.

ये हि वृत्तिं विजानन्ति ज्ञात्वापि वर्द्धयन्ति ये ।
ते वै सत्पुरुषा धन्या वन्द्यास्ते भुवनत्रये ॥१३१॥

131. Hail to those, happy and virtuous beings who, on the other hand, know this state and knowing it grow perfect in it by constant practice. Respect is due to them at the hands of all the three worlds.

येषां वृत्तिः समा वृद्धा परिपक्वा च सा पुनः ।
ते वै सद्ब्रह्मतां प्राप्ता नेतरे शब्दवादिनः ॥१३२॥

132. Those who have reached to the perfection of this state of *Brahma*, and have thoroughly mastered it, the ever-existent, are *Brahma* itself; and not those who merely talk glibly about the matter.

कुशला ब्रह्मवार्त्तायां वृत्तिहीनाः सुरागिणः ।
तेऽप्यज्ञानितया नूनं पुनरायान्ति यान्ति च ॥१३३॥

133. Those again who are clever at talking about *Brahma*, but are void of any real attempt towards reaching to that state and are fast bound to the ties of transitory pleasures,—have to pass and repass (in various births). in consequence of this their hypocrisy and ignorance.

निमेषार्द्धं न तिष्ठन्ति वृत्तिं ब्रह्ममयीं विना ।
यथा तिष्ठन्ति ब्रह्माद्याः सनकाद्याः शुकादयः ॥१३४॥

134. (The enlightened) never remain even for a minute, without uniting their souls with *Brahma*: as did Brahma, Sanakádika, Shuka and other *Mahátmas*.

कार्ये कारणताऽयाता कारणेन हि कार्यता ।
कारणत्वं ततो गच्छेत्कार्याभावे विचारतः ॥१३५॥

135. The cause is reflected in the effect but not the effect in the cause. Hence well-directed thought will prove that on account of the relative non-existence of the effect in the cause the cause itself also could hardly be called the cause of that effect; i.e. must vanish as the active instrumental cause of anything—but should ever stand by itself—all existence, all intelligence and all joy.

अथ शुद्धं भवेद्वस्तु यद्वै वाचामगोचरम् ।
द्रष्टव्यं मृद्घटेनैव दृष्टान्तेन पुनःपुनः ॥१३६॥

136. Thus there will remain that effulgent universal essence, which transcends both mind and speech. This should repeatedly be studied from such ordinary illustrations as of earth and the jar made of it &c.

अनेनैव प्रकारेण वृत्तिर्ब्रह्मात्मिका भवेत् ।
उदेति शुद्धचित्तानां वृत्तिज्ञानं ततःपरम् ॥१३७॥

137. Perseverance in this direction brings about, in those whose minds are sufficiently enlightened, the state of constant knowledge which ultimately leads to its spontaneous and natural unification with *Brahma.*

कारणं व्यतिरेकेण पुमानादौ विलोकयेत् ।
अन्वयेन पुनस्तद्धि कार्ये नित्यं प्रपश्यति ॥१३८॥

138. Every student should first contemplate and grasp the cause as existing apart from its effect; he would then constantly see by inseparable relation the cause in the effect.

कार्ये हि कारणं पश्येत्पश्चात्कार्यं विसर्जयेत् ।
कारणत्वं ततोगच्छेदवशिष्टं भवेन्मुनिः ॥१३९॥

139. Thus having contemplated the cause as reflected in the effect, the effect must be entirely dismissed (from the

mind). When this is done, the cause will cease to be such, and what will remain will be the ever existent, ever conscious, all pervading indescribable *Brahma.*

भावितं तीव्रवेगेन यद्वस्तु निश्चयात्मना ।
पुमांस्तद्धि भवेच्छीघ्रं ज्ञेयं भ्रमरकीटवत् ॥१४०॥

140. A man becomes that on which he resolutely and persistently thinks. This we infer from the ordinary illustration of the bee and the worm.*

अदृश्यं भावरूपं च सर्वमेव चिदात्मकम् ।
सावधानतया नित्यं स्वात्मानं भावयेद्बुधः ॥१४१॥

141. All this universe visible or invisible, (implying the triad of the seer, seen and sight) is one eternal consciousness.

दृश्यं ह्यदृश्यतां नीत्वा ब्रह्माकारेण चिंतयेत् ।
विद्वान् नित्यसुखे तिष्ठेद्धिया चिद्रसपूर्णया ॥१४२॥

142. The enlightened should always look upon the universe as one in and of Brahma, by resolving the visible into the invisible;—thus will he, through his mind being ever filled with the bliss of identifying himself with this universal consciousness, easily attain to the condition of eternal happiness.

एभिरङ्गैः समायुक्तो राजयोग उदाहृतः ।
किंचित्पक्वकषायाणां हठयोगेन संयुतः ॥१४३॥

143. This with the parts set forth above is *Rája* or mental *yoga* mixed with *Hatha* or physical *Yoga* prescribed for those who have already lost great portion of their taste for the pleasures of the senses.

---

* The bee takes hold of any small worm and even while it is alive puts it into a small whole of clay specially prepared, and blocks up the opening. The worm thinking in its dark prison of the bee and bee alone, remains there till the bee returning at its proper time, removes the clay and with it a sting awakens the worm which immediately flies out another bee incarnate.

परिपक्वं मनो येषां केवलोऽयं च सिद्धिदः ।
गुरुदैवतभक्तानां सर्वेषां सुलभो जवात् ॥ १४४ ॥

144. To those whose mind is completely ripe (by विवेक वैराग्य &c.) this (Rája Yoga) alone (without any *Hatha* or physical yoga) is useful; this *yoga* again being one easily accessible even to those who are devoted to their teachers, or to their favourite gods, &c

इति श्रीपरमहंसपरिव्राजकाचार्यश्रीमच्छङ्करभगवता
विरचिताऽपरोक्षाऽनुभूतिः समाप्ता ।

DISCRIMINATION OF SPIRIT AND NOT SPIRIT.

(Translated from the original Sanskrit of Śankarácharyá.)

BY MOHINEE M. CHATTERJEE, F.T.S.

[An apology is scarcely needed for undertaking, a translation of Sankaracharya's celebrated Synopsis of Vedantism entitled "Atmánátma Vivekah." This little treatise, within a small compass, fully sets forth the scope and purpose of the Vedanta philosophy. It has been a matter of no little wonder, considering the authorship of this pamphlet and its own intrinsic merits, that a translation of it has not already been executed by some competent scholar. The present translation, though pretending to no scholarship, is dutifully literal except, however, the omission of a few lines relating to the etymology of the words शरीर (Sarira) and देह (Deha) and one or two other things which, though interesting in themselves have no direct bearing on the main subject of treatment. Some other passages in the text have also, for the convenience of readers, been removed to an appendix at the end.—Tr.]

Nothing is Spirit which can be perceived by the senses. To one possessed of right discrimination, the Spirit is like a thing perceptible. This right discrimination of Spirit and Not-spirit is set forth in millions of treatises.

The discrimination of Spirit and Not-spirit is given (below) :—

Q. Whence comes pain to the Spirit?

A. By reason of its taking a body. It is said in the Sruti* : "Not in this (state of existence) is there cessation of pleasure and pain of a living thing possessed of a body."

* Chandogya Upanishat.—Tr.

Q. By what is produced this taking of a body ?

A. By *Karma.**

Q. Why does it become so by *Karma* ?

A. By desire and the rest (*i. e.*, the passions.)

Q. By what are desire and the rest produced ?

A. By egoism (अभिमान :).

Q. By what again is egoism produced ?

A. By want of right discrimination.

Q. By what is this want of right discrimination produced ?

A. By ignorance (अज्ञानं).

Q. Is ignorance produced by anything ?

A. No, by nothing. Ignorance is without beginning and ineffable by reason of its being the intermingling of the real (सत्) and the unreal (असत्).† It is a something embodying the three qualities ‡ and is said to be opposed to Wisdom in as much as it produces the concept "I am ignorant." The Sruti says, " (Ignorance), is the power of the Deity and is enshrouded by its own qualities."§

The origin of pain can thus be traced to ignorance and it will not cease until ignorance is entirely dispelled, which will be only when the identity of the Self with Brahma (the Universal Spirit) is fully realized.‖ Anticipating the conten-

---

* This word, it is impossible to translate. It means the doing of a thing for the attainment of an object of worldly desire.—Tr.

† This word, as used in *Vaidantic* works, is generally misunderstood. It does not mean the negation of everything ; it means "that which does not exhibit the Truth," the "illusory."

यदसच्छब्देनाभिधानं तदव्याकृतत्वाभिप्रायं न तु अत्यंताभावाभिप्रायं ।
Adhikarana Mála (note)—Tr.

‡ *Satva* (goodness), *Rajas* (foulness) and *Tamas* (darkness) are the three qualities.

§ Chandogya Upanishat.—Tr.

‖ This portion has been condensed from the original.—Tr.

tion that the eternal acts (*i. e.*, those enjoined by the Vedas,) are proper and would lead to the destruction of ignorance therefore it is said that ignorance cannot be dispelled by *Karma.* Then—

Q. What comes of such acts?

A. Conflict of Wisdom and *Karma.* Therefore it is clear that Ignorance can only be removed by Wisdom.

Q. How can this Wisdom be acquired?

A. By discussion—by discussing as to the nature of Spirit and Not-spirit.

Q. Who are worthy of engaging in such discussion?

A. Those who have acquired the four qualifications.

Q. What are the four qualifications?

A. (1), True discrimination of permanent and impermanent things. (2), Indifference to the enjoyment of the fruits of one's actions both here and hereafter. (3), Possession of *Sama* and the other five qualities. (4), An intense desire of becoming liberated (from material existence).

(1.) *Q.* What is the right discrimination of permanent and impermanent things?

A. Certainly as to the Material Universe being false, and illusive and Brahma being the only reality.

(2.) Indifference to the enjoyment of the fruits of one's actions in this world is to have the same amount of disinclination for the enjoyment of worldly objects of desire (such as garland of flowers, sandalwood paste women and the like) beyond those absolutely necessary for the preservation of life, as one has for vomited food, &c. The same amount of disinclination to enjoyment in the society of Rhambha, Urvasi and other celestial nymphs in the higher spheres of life beginning with *Svarga loka* and ending with *Brahma loka.**

---

* These, it is supposed, include the whole range of *Rupa loka* (the world of forms) in Buddhistic esoteric philosophy.—Tr.

(3.) *Q.* What are the six qualities beginning with *Sama* ?

A. *Sama, Dama, uparati, titikshá, samádhana* and *sraddhá.* *Sama* is the repression of the inward sense called *Manas, i.e.,* not allowing it to engage in any other thing but *Sravana* (listening to what the sages say about the spirit), *Manana* * (reflecting on it), *Nididhyasana* (meditating on the same). *Dama* is the repression of the external senses.

Q. What are the external senses ?

A. The five organs of perception and the five bodily organs for the performance of external acts. Restraining these from all other things but *Sravana* and the rest—is *dama.*

Uparati is the abstaining on principle from engaging in any of the acts and ceremonies enjoined by the *shastras.* Otherwise it is the state of the mind which is always engaged in *Sravana* and the rest, without ever diverging from them.

Titikshá (literally the desire to leave) is the bearing with indifference all opposites (such as pleasure and pain, heat and cold, &c.). Otherwise, it is the showing of forbearance to a person one is capable of punishing.

Whenever a mind, engaged in *Sravana* and the rest, wanders to any worldly object of desire, and, finding it worthless, returns to the performance of the three exercises—such returning is called *samadhána.*

Sraddhá is an intensely strong faith in the utterances of one's *guru* and of the Vedanta philosophy.

(4.) An intense desire for liberation is called *mumukshatvam.*

Those who possess these four qualifications, are worthy of engaging in discussions as to the nature of Spirit and Not-spirit, and, like Brahmacharins, they have no other duty (but such discussion). It is not, however, at all improper for householders to engage in such discussions ; but, on the contrary,

* These terms will be more fully explained in the appendix.—Tr.

such a course is highly meritorious. For it is said :—Whoever, with due reverence, engages in the discussion of subjects treated of in *Vedanta* philosophy and does proper service to his *guru*, reaps happy fruits. Discussion as to the nature of Spirit and Not-spirit is therefore a duty.

Q. What is Spirit ?

A. It is that principle which enters into the composition of man besides the *three bodies*, and which is distinct from the five sheaths (*Koshas*), being *sat* (existence),* *chit* (consciousness),† and *ananda* (bliss),‡ and witness of the *three states*.

Q. What are the three bodies ?

A. The gross (*sthula*), the subtile *sukshama* and the causal (*kàrana*).

Q. What is the *gross body* ?

A. That which is the effect of the *Mahabhutas* (primordial subtile elements) differentiated into the five gross ones (*Panchikrita*),¶ is born of *Karma* and subject to the six changes beginning with birth.§ It is said :—

What is produced by the (subtile) elements differentiated into the five gross ones, is acquired by *Karma*, and is the measure of pleasure and pain, is called the body (*sarira*) *par excellence.*

---

* This stands for *Purusha.—Tr.*

† This stands for *Prakriti*, cosmic matter, irrespective of the state we perceive it to be in.—*Tr.*

‡ Bliss is *Màyà* or *Sakti*, it is the creative energy producing changes of state in *Prakriti*. Says the Shruti (Taittiriya Upanishat) :—" Verily from Bliss are all these *bhutas* born, and being born by it they live, and they return and enter into Bliss."—*Tr.*

¶ The five subtile elements thus produce the gross ones :—each of the five is divided into eight parts, four of those parts and one part of each of the others enter into combination, and the result is the gross element corresponding with the subtile element, whose parts predominate in the composition.-*Tr.*

§ These six changes are :—birth, death, being in time, growth, decay, and undergoing change of substance (*parinàm*) as milk is changed into whey.—*Tr.*

Q. What is the *subtile body*?

A. It is the effect of the elements not differentiated into five and having 17 characterstic marks (*lingas*).

Q. What are the seventeen?

A. The five channels of knowledge (*Jnanendriyas*), the five *organs of action*, the five *vital airs* beginning with *prána*, and *manas* and *buddhi*.

Q. What are the *Jnanendriyas*?

A. [Spiritual] Ear, skin, eye, tongue and nose.

Q. What is the *ear*?

A. That channel of knowledge which transcends the [physical] ear, is limited by the auricular orifice on which the *ákás* depends, and which is capable of taking cognisance of sound.

Q. The *skin*?

A. That which transcends the skin, on which the skin depends, and which extends from head to foot and has the power of perceiving heat and cold.

Q. The *eye*?

A. That which transcends the ocular orb, on which the orb depends, which is centred in the black iris and has the power of cognising forms.

Q. The *tongue*?

A. That which transcends the tongue and can perceive taste.

Q. The *nose*?

A. That which transcends the nose, and has the power of smelling.

Q. What are the *organs of action*?

A. The organ of speech (vách), hands, feet, etc.

Q. What is *vách*?

A. That which transcends speech, in which speech resides, and which is located in *eight different centres** and has the power of speech.

Q. What are the *eight centres?*

A. Breast, throat, head, upper and neither lips, palate, ligature (frenum), binding the tongue to the lower jaw and tongue.

Q. What is the *organ of the hands?*

A. That which transcends the hands on which the palms depend and which has the power of giving and taking. * * * (The other organs are similarly described).

Q. What is the *antahkarana?*†

A. *Manas, buddhi, chitta* and *ahankara* form it. The seat of the *manas* is the root of the throat, of *buddhi* the face, of *chitta* the umbilicus, and of *ahankara* the breast. The functions of these four components of *antahkarana* are respectively doubt, certainty, retention, and egotism.

Q. How are the five vital airs,‡ beginning with *prana*, named?

A. *Prána, apána, vyána, udana* and *samána.* Their locations are said to be:—of *prana* the breast, of *apana* the fundamentum,

* The secret *commentaries* say seven; for it does not separate the lips into the "upper" and "nether" lips. And it adds to the seven centres the *seven* passages in the head connected with, and effected by, *vách*; namely—the mouth, the two eyes, the two nostrils and the two ears. "The left year, eye and nostril being the messengers *of the right side of the head*; the right ear, eye and nostril—those of the left side." Now this is purely scientific. The latest discoveries and conclusions of modern physiology have shown that the power or the faculty of human speech is located in the third frontal cavity of the left hemisphere of the brain. On the other hand, it is a well known fact that the nerve tissues inter-cross each other (decussate) in the brain in such a way that the motions of our left extremeties are governed by the right hemisphere, while the motions of our right hand limbs are subject to the left hemisphere of the brain.—*Ed.*

† A flood of light will be thrown on the text by an editorial note in *Theosophist*, vol. IV, 11, 269:—"*Antahkarana* is the path of communication between soul and body, entirely disconnected with the former, existing with, belonging to, and dying with the body." This path is well traced in the text. —*Tr.*

‡ These vital airs and sub-airs are magnetic currents.—*Tr.*

of *samána*, the umbilicus, of *udána* the throat, and *vyána* is spread all over the body. Functions of these are :—*prána* goes out, *apána* descends, *udána* ascends, *samána* reduces the food eaten into an undistinguishable state, and *vyána* circulates all over the body. Of these five vital airs there are five sub-airs, namely, *nága*, *kúrma*, *krikara*, *devadatta* and *dhananjaya*. Functions of these are :—erructations produced by *nága*, *kúrma* opens the eye, *dhananjaya* assimilates food, *devadatta* causes yawning, and *krikara* produces appetite—this is said by those versed in *Yoga*.

The presiding powers of the five channels of knowledge and the others are *dik* (akás'a) and the rest. *Dik*, *váta* (air), *arka* (sun), *prachetá* (water), Aswini, *bahni* (fire), Indra, Upendra, Mrityu (death), *Chandra* (moon), *Brahma*, *Rudra*, and *Kshetrajnesvara*,* which is the great Creator and cause of everything. These are the presiding powers of ear, and the others in the order in which they occur.

All these taken together form the *linga s'arira*.† It is also said in the *Sastras* :—

The five vital airs, *manas*, *buddhi*, and the ten organs form the subtile body, which arises from the subtile elements, undifferentiated into the five gross ones, and which is the means of the perception of pleasure and pain.

Q. What is the *Kárana s'arira* ?‡

A. It is ignorance (*avidyá*), which is the cause of the other

---

* For an explanation of this term See S'ankara's commentaries on the *Brahma Sútras*.—*Tr*.

† *Linga* means that which conveys meaning, characteristic mark.

‡ Mr. Subba Row understands it in exactly the same way. See *Theosophist*, Vol. IV, 10, 249. See also in this connection an editorial note in the same number of that journal, p. 255, running thus :—

"This *Karana s'arira* is often mistaken by the uninitiated for *Linga s'arira* (*e. g.* Sridhara Swami in his commentaries on the *Bhagvat Gitá*—Tr.) and since it is described as the inner rudimentary or latent embryo of the body—confounded with it."

I am under the impression that I follow the best authorities in regarding *Kàrana s'arira* as surviving in *devachan*, and when the proper time comes, furnishing the monad with the other two bodies, of which it embodies the causal germs.—*Tr*.

two bodies, and which is without beginning,* ineffable, reflection [of Brahma] and productive of the concept of non-identity between self and Brahma. It is also said :—

" Without a beginning, ineffable *avidyá* is called the *upádhi* (vehicle)—*kárana* (cause). Know the Spirit to be truly different from the three *upádhis i. e.*, bodies.

Q. What is *Not-Spirit* ?

A. It is the three bodies [described above], which are impermanent, inanimate (*jada*), essentially painful and subject to congregation and segregation.

Q. What is *impermanent* ?

A. That which does not exist in one and the same state in the three divisions of time [namely, present, past and future.]

Q. What is *inanimate* (jada)?

A. That which cannot distinguish between the objects of its own cognition and the objects of the cognition of others.

* * * *

Q. What are the three states [mentioned above as those of which the Spirit is witness] ?

A. Wakefulness (*jágrata*), dreaming (*svapna*), and the state of dreamless slumber, (*sushupti*).

Q. What is the state of *wakefulness* ?

A. That in which objects are known through the avenue of [physical] senses.

Q. Of *dreaming* ?

A. That in which objects are perceived by reason of desires resulting from impressions produced during wakefulness.

Q. What is the state of *dreamless slumber* ?

A. That in which there is an utter absence of the perception of objects.

---

* It must not be supposed that *avidyá* is here confounded with *prakriti*. What is meant by *avidyá* being without beginning, is that it forms no link in the *Karmic* chain leading to succession of births and deaths, it is evolved by a law embodied in *prakriti* itself.—*Tr.*

The in-dwelling of the notion of "I" in the gross body during wakefulness is *vis'va* (world of objects),* in subtle body during dreaming is *taijas* (magnetic fire), and in the causal body during dreamless slumber is *prájna* (One life.)

Q. What are the five sheaths?

A. *Annamaya*, *Pránamaya*, *Manomaya*, *Vijnánamaya*, and *Anandamaya*.†

Annamaya is the transformation of *anna* ‡ (food), *pránamaya* of *prána* (life), *Manomaya* of *manas*, *Vijnánamaya* of *vijnána* (finite perception), *Ánandamaya* of *ananda* (illusive bliss).

Q. What is the *Annamaya* sheath?

A. The gross body.

Q. Why?

A. The food eaten by father and mother is transformed into semen and blood, the combination of which is transformed into the shape of a body. It wraps up like a sheath and hence so called. It is the transformation of food and wraps up the spirit like a sheath—it shows the spirit which is infinite as finite, which is without the six changes beginning with birth as subject to those changes which is without the three kinds of pain¶ as liable to them. It conceals the spirit as the sheath conceals the sword, the husk the grain, or the womb the fœtus.

Q. What is the next sheath?

A. The combination of the five organs of action, and the five vital airs form the *Pránamaya* sheath.

---

* That is to say, by mistaking the gross body for self, the consciousness of external objects is produced.—*Tr.*

† This subject is also treated of by the author in the *Atmabodha* and has been admirably expounded in this journal for July last, p. 255, q. v.—*Tr.*

‡ This word also means the earth in Sanskrit.—*Tr.*

¶ The three kinds of pain are:—

Adhibhautika, i. e., from external objects, *e. g.*, from thieves, wild animals, &c.

Ádhidaivika, i. e., from elements, *e. g.*, thunder, &c.

Ádhyàtmika, i. e., from within one's self, *e. g.* head-ache, &c. See *Sànkhya Kàrikà*, Gaudapada's commentary to the opening Sloká.—*Tr.*

By the manifestation of *prána*, the spirit which is speechless appears as if the speaker, which never gives as the giver, which never moves as if in motion, which is devoid of hunger and thirst as if hungry and thirsty.

Q. What is the third sheath?

A. It is the five (subtile) organs of sense (*jnánendriya*) and *manas.*

By the manifestation of this sheath (*vikára*) the spirit which is devoid of doubt appears as doubting, devoid of grief and delusion as if grieved and deluded, devoid of sight as if seeing.

Q. What is the *Vijnánmaya* sheath?

A. [The essence of] tho five organs of sense form this sheath in combination with *buddhi.*

Q. Why is this sheath so called the *jiva* (personal ego), which by reason of its thinking itself the actor, enjoyer, &c., goes to the other *loka* and comes back to this?*

A. It wraps up and shows the spirit which never acts as the actor, which never cognises as conscious which has no concept of certainty as being certain, which is as never evil or inanimate as being both.

Q. What is the *Ánandamaya* sheath?

A. It is the *antahkarana,* wherein ignorance predominates and which produces gratification, enjoyment etc.

It wraps up and shows the spirit, which is void of desire, enjoyment and fruition as having them, which has no conditioned happiness as being possessed thereof.

Q. Why is the spirit said to be different from the three bodies?

A. That which is truth cannot be untruth, consciousness inanimate, bliss misery, or *vice versa.*

Q. Why is it called the witness of the three states?

A. Being the master of the three states, it is the knowledge of the three states, as existing in the present, past and future.†

* That is to say, first from birth to birth.—*Tr*

† It is the stable basis upon which the three states arise and disappear. —*Tr.*

Q. How is the spirit different from the five sheaths?

A. This is being illustrated by an example :—

"This is my cow," "this is my calf," "this is my son or daughter," "this is my wife," "this is my *ánandamaya* sheath," and so on*—the spirit can never be connected with these concepts; it is different from and witness of them all. For it is said in the Upanishat :—

[The spirit is] "naught of sound, of touch, of form, or colour of taste, or of smell; it is everlasting, having no beginning or end, superior [in order of involution] to *Prakriti*,† whoever correctly understands it as such attains *mukti* (liberation.)"

The spirit has been called [above] *sat*, *chit* and *ánanda*.

Q. What is meant by its being *sat* (existence)?

A. Existing unchanged in the three divisions of time and uninfluenced by anything else.

Q. What by being *chit* (consciousness)?

A. Manifesting itself without depending upon anything else and containing the germ of everything in itself.

Q. What by being *ánanda* (bliss)?

A. The *ne plus ultra* of bliss.

Whoever knows without doubt and apprehension of its being otherwise, his self as one with Brahma, which its eternal, non-dual and unconditioned, attains *moksha*.

APPENDIX.

I.

In the opening Sloka all *drisya* is described as *anátma* (not spirit) and the spirit of one possessed of right discrimination is called *drik*. These two Sanscrit words are thus described in the author's *Brahma námávalimálá* or the String of names of Brahma, Sloka 18 :—"*Drisya* and *drik* exist, different from each other; the former is *máyá* and the latter Brahma—this is celebrated in all Vedantic works."

---

* The "heresy of individuality" or *attaváda* of the Buddhists.—*Tr.*

† Differentiated matter.

II.

S'arira (body) is derived from the root *s'ri*, to shrink, and is called because it shrinks with age or when the knowledge of identity of self with Brahma is realised.

Deha (body) is from the root *dah*, to burn, so called on account of its being burnt up after death or at all events by the three-fold pain in life (*vide supra*)

THE ÁTMABODHA OF SRIMAT S'ANKARÁCHÁRYA.

(Translated from the Sanskrit by B. P. Narasimmiah, F. T. S.)

THE plan adopted in the following translation is, that the marginal numbers shall denote the respective numbers of the slokams in the original, and that the rendering shall be as literal and verbatim as possible.

1. The work called ÁTMABODHA, which is desired by religious observers, and by sinless and dispassionate seekers after *Moksham*, will now be written.

2. *Question*:—Of so many ways to Moksham, why should knowledge, or wisdom, or *Gnyánam* alone be the chief?

Answer:—That relationship which exists between the fuel, &c., and the fire itself, in the culinary process, exists also between *Tapas, &c.*, which are the several means of attaining *Moksham, i. e., Nirvána* and *Gnyánam* itself. As fire is the most important of all the materials necessary for cooking, so *Gnyanam* is the most important of all the means for attaining Moksham.

3. *Ques*:—*Karma, i. e.,* ritual, has got wonderful power. While a small portion of such *Karma* can wash off all *Agnyánam* or darkness, how is *Gnyánam* necessary?

Ans:—Since *Agnyánam* and *Karma* are not hostile to each other, the latter cannot destroy the former, *e. g.*, as dirt cannot wash off dirt, so no amount of such *Karma* or ritualistic observances can dispel that (spiritual) darkness—*Agnyánam*. But

Gnyánam or Light (spiritual) alone, which is self-shining, can remove *Agnyánam* as the Sun drives off his opponent Darkness,

4. *Ques*:—How is it possible to attribute *Kevalatvam, i. e.* Oneness, to *Átmá* which appears as different in different, individuals?

Ans:—The sun is far away from the clouds, and is larger than the largest of them all. Still each patch of a cloud, screening the sun from us, gives him a distorted and a special aspect. This distortion and difference in appearance is due, not to the sun who is all-shining and has a uniform existence, but to the nature of such clouds. And no sooner the clouds vanish than the orb of light is seen to be one and the same. This analogy holds good in the case of *Átmá* peeping out through so many loop-holes of bodies. When the cloud-like *Agnyánam* or spiritual darkness disappears, that one *Átmá* shines everywhere.

5. *Ques*:—How can *Átmá* have the quality of oneness, *i. e* non-duality, inasmuch as he has the knowledge of actions, which knowledge establishes *Dvaitam* or duality?

Ans:—The knowledge of things in their true light (*Vastu-tatwa-gnyánam*), liberating *Jiva* from the fetters of ignorance, renders it pure, and dies away with that fetter-like ignorance, just as the particles of the water-purifying seed sink down with the sediment which they separate from the impure water in the process of purifying the same.

6. *Ques*:—How can one consistently deny the reality of this worldly life, this material existence, this *samsáram*, while we are enjoying it?

Ans. Just as a dream, which seems to us to be a reality while we are dreaming, is not so after waking, so the world of pride—*Ahankára-prapancham*—which is *samsáram*, to one who is blinded by love and hatred, appears to be all real or substantial so long as that one is involved in it, or enamoured of it; but no longer so after the acquisition of true knowledge or *Gnyánam*.

7. So long as the All-supporting *Adrayam*—non-dual—Brahma is not recognized, so long this world is belived in as a reality as mistakeably as one who discovers the real silver in the brightness of a pearl-shell.

8. As the water bubbles rise, exist, and burst in an ocean, so the worlds appear, exist, and disappear in *Upádané Paramésvaré* or *Material-cause-like Paramésvara* or God.

9. Although the ornaments are of different shapes, yet they do not differ from gold in their quality; similarly the creatures though of diverse forms, are not different from the Creator—the all-pervading, omnipresent, *Sachchidánanda-svarúpa Átmá.*

10. The Ruler of mind and all other senses., the all-pervading *Paramátma,* under the cloaks of *Sthúla, Sükshma,* and, *Kárana S'ariras,* seems divided. This divided appearance ceases with the destruction of such cloaks. This is like the bits of the Akas'as of different vessels, or finite spaces, becoming commingled with the universal Aka'sa, or Infinite Space, suchwhen vessels are destroyed.

11. As to the water itself, which is naturally white and sweet, the qualities of bitterness, yellowness, &c., resulting from its contact with differnt soils, are attributed; so, to *Atmá* who is *Sachchidànanda* and who is casteless, nameless, and professionless, are assigned some caste, name, and profession, only through the *Upádhis*—or causes or under the colour—of *Sthúla Súkshma*, and *Karma S'ariras.*

12. *Sthúla S'ariram*:—is that which is made up of five-foldly sub-divided five grand elements of Earth, Water, Fire, Air, and Akà'sa or Ether, which is the creature of *Agami Sanchita Prárabdha Karma* and which is the seat of the enjoyment of pleasure and pain, joy and sorrow.

The Method of Panchikarnam.

Panchikaranam means the mixing together of the five-fold, sub-divisional parts of each of the five grand elements, viz. Earth, Water, &c.

The process of such mixture :—

Of the five grand elements, divide each into two parts, keep one part separate, and divide the other part into four sub-divisional parts; and the blending together of each of these four sub-divisional parts successively with one sub-divisional part at a time of every other grand element is what forms *Panchkaranam.* For instance, divide the Earth element into two parts; keep aloof one part, and sub-divide the second part into four parts again. Without mixing these four sub-divisional parts with the first part of the earth element already set apart, you must mix each of these sub-divisional parts with one sub-divisional part, at a time, of every *other* grand element (Here earth element is excluded).

The following table of Panchikaranam is intended to illustrate in detail the names of *Manas,* &c., resulting from the said process of mixture :—

TABLE OF PANCHIKARANAM.

Atma.				
Akasam. (Air or Ether) Anthâh-karanam.	Manas.	Buddhi.	Chittam.	Ahankâram.
Samâna-vâyuvu.	*Wâyuvu.* (Wind) Vyânavâ-yuvau.	Udânavayuvu.	Pranâvayuvu.	Apânavâyuvu.
Srotrêndriyam. The sense of Hearing or Ear.	Twagêndriyam The sense of Touch or Skin.	*Têjas.* (Fire.) Chakshurendri-yam. The sense of Sight or Eyes	Jihwendriyam. The sense of Taste or Tongue.	Ghrânên-driyam. The sense of Smelling or Nose.
Sabda. Sound.	Sparsa. Touch.	Rupa. Shape or Form.	*Apah.* (Water.) Rasa. Taste.	Gandha. Smell.
Vâgendriyan. The sense of Speech or Month.	Panindriyam. The sense of Handling or Hands.	Pâdêndriyam. The sense of Feet or Feet.	Pâyvindriyam. The sense of Excretion or Excretory Organs.	*Prithvi.* (Earth.) Oopastên-driyam. The sense of generating or Generative Organs.

THE EXEMPLIFICATION OF AKASAM.

The description of the *Tatwams*, resulting from the commingling of fourfold-divisional parts of Akàsam and one sub-divisional part at a time of every other grand element than Akàsam, is as follows :—

(*a*). From the union of one of the four sub-divisional parts of Akàsam and one sub-divisional part of Earth or Matter, sprang *Ahankáram*.

(*b*). By a similar process of the union of a part of Akásam and a part of Water, resulted *Chittam*.

(*c*). A part of Akásam and a part of Fire together produced *Buddhi*.

(*d*). A part of Akàsam with a part of Wind or Vàyuvu yielded *Manas*.

The first and unsubdivided portion of Akásam became *Anthâhkaranam*.

THE EXEMPLIFICATION OF VAYUVU.

(*a*). On the similar process as above
a part of Vàyuvu + a part of Earth = *Apánaváyuvu*.
(*b*). Do. + do. Water = *Pránaváyuvu*.
(*c*). Do. + do. Fire = *Udánaváyuvu*.
(*d*). Do. + do. Akàsam = *Samanáváyuvu*.

The unsubdivided first half of Vàyuvu became *Vyánaváyuváu*.

THE EXEMPLIFICATION OF FIRE.

(*a*). On the above process
a part of Fire + a part of Earth = *Ghranendriyam*. — The sense of Smell.

(*b*). A part of Fire + a part of water = *Jiwhendriyam*.— The sense of Taste.

(*c*). Do. + do. Vàyuvu = *Twagendriyam*.— The sense of Touch.

(*d*). Do. + do. Akása = *Srotrendriyam*.— The sense of Hearing.

The unsubdivided half of Fire became *Chakshurendriyam.*—The sense of Sight.

THE EXEMPLIFICATION OF WATER.

(a). On the same process

a part of Water + a part of Earth = *Gandha.*—Smell.

(b). Do. + do. Fire = *Rupa.*—Form or Shape.

(c). Do. + do. Váyuvu = *Sparsa.*—Touch.

(d). Do. + do. Akàsa = *Sabda.*—Sound.

The unsubdivided half of Water became *Rasa.*—Taste.

THE EXEMPLIFICATION OF EARTH OR MATTER.

(a). Again on the same process a part of

Earth or Matter + a part of Water = *Páyvindriyam.*—The sense of Excretory Organs.

(b). Do. + do. Fire—*Padendriyam.*—The sense of Feet.

(c). Do. + do. Váyuvu—*Panindriyam.*—The sense of Hands.

(d). Do. + do. Akása—*Vagéndriyam.*—The sense of Speech.

The unsubdivided half of Earth element became *Oopasten driyam.*—The sense of Generating or Generative Organs.

The group of Panchikaranam (Panchikaranakadambam):—

I. Anthåhkaranam, Samánaváyuvu, Srotendriyam (The sense of Hearing, or Ear), Sabda (Sound), and Vágéndriyam (The sense of Speech, or Mouth)—these five form the Group of Akásam or *Akasakadambam.*

II. Manas, Vyánaváyuvu, Twagendriyam (The sense of Touch, or Skin), Sparsa (Touch), and Pánindriyam (The sense of Handling, or Hands)—these five form the Group of Váyuvu or *Váyukdambam.*

III. Buddhi, Udánaváyuvu, Chakshurendriyam (The sense of Sight, or Eyes), Rúpa (Shape or Form), and Pádéndriyam (The sense of Feet, or Feet)—these five form the Group of Fire or *Téjahkadabmam.*

IV. Chittam, Pránavâyuvu, Jiwhendriyam (The sense of Taste, or Tongue), Rasa (Taste), and Páyvindriyam (The sense of Excretion, or Excretory Organs)—these five form the Group of Water or *Jalakadambam.*

V. Ahankáram, Apánavâyuvu, Ghránéndriyam (The sense of Smelling, or The Nose), Gandha (Smell), and Oopastendriyam (The sense of Generating, or Generative Organs)—these five form the group of Earth or Matter or *Prithvikadambam.*

13. *Súkshmasariram* ;—is that which is composed of five vayus (Prána, Apána, Vyána, Udána, and Samána) hesitating Manas, determining Buddhi, and the senses (Touch or Skin, Sight or Eyes, Hearing or Ear, Taste or Tongue, and Smell or Nose ; and speech or Mouth, Hands, Feet, Excretory Organs, and Generative Organs), is born of Smell or Súkshma elements *un*divided into five parts, and is the chief internal seat of the enjoyment of pleasure and pain. In brief, Súkshmasariram is the one internal seat of experiencing that pleasure and pain which is not to be found in Átmá.

14. *Káranadeham* is the prop and support of the other two dehams, viz., Sthúla and Sükshma. The indescribable, the eternal Máya or Avidyá is the means of *Upádhi* which causes the *Stkúla and Sukshma dehams.* But we ought to assure ourselves that that *Upádhi* is quite different from the three Saríras—Sthúla, Sükshma, and Karana; and that *Jiva* itself is made known by *Ahamsabdam.*

15. As a crystal, covered with divers-coloured clothes, is still pure, so the pure Átmá, though enveloped by *five Kosams*, viz., *Annamaya*, *Pranamaya*, *Manomaya*, *Vignyanamaya*, and *Anandamaya* along with Hunger, Thirst, Sorrow, Love, Decripitude, and Death, is still untouched by, unconnected with, and different from, any of those outer sheaths

16. As you separate rice from husk and dust, so by means of *Sravana*, *Manana*, and *Nidhidhyásana*, you should ascertain what is Átmá, and know him to be separate from this body composed of five Kosams.

17. A'kàsam, shapelessly existing everywhere, is reflected only in the pure transparent substances. So also Atma, who is shapeless and is everywhere, is reflected in, and seen by, the pure mind alone, which is not stained with Love, Mòham, &c.

18. Atma, who is separate from Sarìra, Senses, Manas, and Buddhi, and who is an unconcerned witness of the actions of *Anthàhkaranam* which is made up of Manas, Buddhi, Chitta and Ahànkara, must be known as the sovereign who disinterestedly supervises every deed and action of the Vazirs, &c., in obedience to his order.

19. As the Moon, screened by the passing clouds, seems to move, so Atma, covered with the objects of senses, &c., (*Indriya-vishayamulu*) seems to move, and act, with those senses, &c. But the *Mumukshus* or the Aspirants of *moksham* (or Nirvàna) must understand Him otherwise—as unconnected with the action of any such senses,

20. As we attribute blueness, &c., to the sky, so we ignorantly attribute body, senses, qualities and actions, to that *Sachchidananda* A'tmá.

21. The attributes of agent and subject are as falsely attributed te Atma, as the motion of water, wherein the moon is reflected, to the moon herself. This is the outcome of the ignorant mind.

22. Atma is also devoid of *Raga* (Love), *Ichchha* (Desire) *Sukha* (Happiness), and *Duhkha* (Misery), which qualities are the issues of Buddhi, for they are present in *Jagrat* (Wakeful state) and *Swapna* (dreaming state) alone, and absent in *Sushupti* (Sleeping state), *i. e.*, in the absence of Buddhi.

23. Then it is doubted what the characteristic feature or *Swarupa* of Atma is. As light characterises the sun, coolness water, and heat fire; so *Sath*, *Chith*, *Ananda*, *Nitya* and *Nirmalatwa* typify Atma.

24. Jiva, the reflection of Sachchidàtmá, *with* the determining quality of Buddhi, and *without* having any experience of the teaching of Srutis, pretends to recognize things.

25. Atma has no *Vikáram* and Buddhi has no *Gnyanam* at any time. Still Jiva, mistaking itself for manas, &c., regards itself as the doer and observer.

As the iron-ball, becoming one with fire, possesses the qualities of redness and burning; so Atma (to all appearances), becoming one with *Anthahkaranam*, seems falsely to think that He Himself is the doer and the seer; but these latter qualities of doing and seeing do not really exist in him. This is how *Mumukshús* ought to uuderstand Atma.

26. Now, how does A'tmá, imposing upon Himself other qualities, experience pleasure and pain?

As the fear is the necessary consequence of mistaking a rope in darkness for serpent; so the mistaking of A'tmá for Jiva is the source of all pleasure and pain, and the fear of several births and re-births. But the clear knowledge of the distinctions in the two cases is the end of all fears, all miseries, and all births and re-births.

27. Why will not A'tmá be recognized by Buddhi, Chittam, and Manas, which are so close to Him?

The fact is that, as the light enlightens the globes, &c., and shows them out, while these globes, &c., themselves in return cannot enlighten or show out that light; so Atma enlightens and enlivens the Manas, Buddhi, Chittam, Ahankàram, and the senses, but cannot, without Himself, be in return enlightened and enlivened *by* them.

28. When it is said that A'tmá, though not comprehensible by Ahankáram, is still cognization by *Gnyánantaram,* it is replied that there is no *Gnyánantaram* apart from A'tmá.

For, as one light does not require the help of another light to make itself known, so A'tmá, who is but *Gnyánam,* needs not other Gnyánam to know Himself.

29. Then, if A'tmá cannot be known by Buddhi, &c., what are the means of knowing Him? As the decisive word of a lapidary distinguishes a precious stone from a worthless one, so A'tmá is knowable by the help of *Mahávakyams,* i. e., Védas,

which tell us that all the difference between *Kinchidgnyátwa Jivátma* and *Sarvagnyátma Paramátmá* is chimerical, and lies only in disquisition and *not* in the real import of the eternal bliss of *Sushupti*. Cf.—the distinction of largeness and smallness of seas exists only in the presence of shores and disappears in their (shores) absence.

30. So long as one fancies a serpent in a rope, so long is he sunk in that fear; but no sooner does the distinction between rope and serpent creep in, than does the dread of the serpent vanish from one's mind. Therefore, you should know once for all that all the bodies are creatures of *Avidyá* and are subject to decay and death, hunger and thirst, sorrow and love; and that your *Self* is that *Brahma*, who is above all Avidyà, and is not affected by old age, &c.,

31. [Having explained (in Slokams 15—30, both inclusive) *Sravanavidhi* which teaches us by *Vedártham* (the meaning of Vedàs) to see that which is on the other side of our physical sight, *Mananvidhi* is now explained in the following five Slokams, *i. è.*, 31—35, both inclusive.]

It should be known that A'tmà is characterised by "I" because He is different from *Sthùla*, *Sukshma* and *Karana Sarirams*, has not those six changes of *Asti*, *Jayate*, *Vardhate*, *Parinamate*, *Apakshiyate* and *Vinasyate*; and that, because he has no senses, he has therefore no sensations as well.

32. That because Atma has no Manas (has no Prànam, is pure, &c., as Srutis tell us). He has no Sorrow (*Duhkha*), Love (*Raga*), Hatred (*Dwesha*), &c.

33. [What a Chela experiences by the help of a Guru, the author explains in the following three Slokams.]

The author says, "I (Atma) (having no Buddhi) am *Nirgunah*, *i. e.*, have no *Gunams* or attributes; (having no senses), am *Nishkriyah*, *i. e.*, actionless; (having no distinction in all three conditions of *Jágrat* or wakeful state, *Swapna* or dreaming state, and *Sushupti* or sleeping state), am *Nityah*, *i. e.*, everlasting; (having no Manas), am *Nirvikalpah*, *i. e.*, desireless;

(having no connection with anything), am sinless and omnipresent; (having no *Lingadeham* filled with *Shodasakala* or 16 *kalas*), am *Nirvikarah*, *i. e.*, formless; (having no relationship), am *Nityamuktah*, *i. e.*, separate; and (having no Antàhkaranam, the creation of Avidya) am *Nirmalah i. e.*, have no *Ragadirupa Malinyam* or the dirt of Love, Hatred &c.

34. (What is the Swarupam of this A'tmá?) "I, *i. e.*, A'tmá, like A'kásam, am an endless entity pervading the inside and outside of the whole universe; am always impartial and not bound by any ties of affection, &c.; am pure; and, being full and filling everything, am motionless.

35. "I am that very Brahma who is the embodiment of the eternal entity, purity, freedom, oneness, eternal and undivided bliss, non-duality, and that which is endless and indestructible in all the three periods of time."

36. That the grandest desire of the *Mokshik* form can be fulfilled by *Sravana* and *Manana*, is explained by *Nidhidhyàsana*.

The constant practice of thinking, in the aforesaid ways, of one-self becoming Brahma, destroys the powers of *Avaranam* and *Viskhepa*, both of *Mayic* origin, as the best medicine cures a disease.

37. (To practise this Yoga or what is said above, certain necessary methods and conditions will be explained.)

Sitting in a solitary place, being desireless, curbing passions, fixing Buddhi upon nothing eles than A'tmà, one should meditate upon the identification of one-self with that A'tmá who is one and *Anantam*, *i. e.*, has no distinction of place, time and things.

38. In response to the question, which naturally suggests itself, viz., "How is it correct to assert the oneness of A'tmá while this perceptible world exists in *Jàgradvaksta?*"—it is said that one, possessing pure Antãhkaranam or internal sense (in other words mind), immersing this perceptible universe in A'tmá, must always meditate upon one's identification with that A'tmá who is like clear sky or A'kasá.

39. [Now it will be told how to reject this world as the creation of *Avidya* and how to ascertain that one-self is Atma.]

One, that has the knowledge of the real nature of things, rejecting everything that pertains only to shape, class, &c., as the child of Avidya, will assume that form which fills all space and possesses *Sat, Chit,* and *Anandam*; in brief, will become Atma Himself.

40. Again, it may be asked, "How can the oneness of Atma be asserted while the existence of *Triputi* is quite palpable?"

In reply, it is said that, since Atma is the embodiment of *Chit, Ananda,* and *Ekatwam or Kevalarupi,* the differences of Triputibhavams cannot creep in; and that Atma is self-refulgent and self-shining.

41. [From the 37th—40th Slokams (both inclusive) *Manana Niyamam* was explained. Now the obvious result of meditating upon that pure Atma will be told.]

According to the above process, by incessant *Dhyanam* or meditation in *Antáhkaranam,* Gnyànam is created; which Gnyànam will, like fire, burn to ashes the whole world of Agnyànam.

42. Here it is stated that, as the identity and unification of Jiva and Atma is known, the Avidyaic belief that himself is body, senses, &c., will vanish; and one will see in one-self that undivided and indivisible Atma.

As, when dawn expels the previous darkness, the sun shines most brilliantly; so, after *Gnyanam* dispels *Agnyanam* or mental darkness, the sun-like Atma shines like a glorious light.

43. [While Atma is always glowing in the form of Gnyánam, how is it consistent to say that He cannot be approached during the period of Agnyànam, but only by the help of Gnyànam, after a time? This seeming inconsistency is removed by the following illustrative explanation.]

Just as the wearer of a neck-lace is unconscious of it—the tangible real thing—when his mind is directed away from it or is engaged upon something else than the neck-lace, and to him it is practically not existing only when his mind is brought to bear upon it; so also the *wiping-off of Avidya or Agnyánam*, which is Gnyànam itself, enables one to know Atma.

44. [How is it right to assert the identity of Jiva and Atma, while it is natural for Jiva to have a separate existence from Atma?]

The same delusion, which creates a thief out of the trunk of a tree in the dead of night, leads us also to fancy the attributes or essence of Jiva in the Omnipresent Brahma. But, when the true nature of Jiva is known, the essence of Jiva ceases to be seen in Brahma.

45. As the sun-rise helps a man, groping his way in utter darkness, and ignorant of sides and directions; so Gnyànam, resulting from the practical knowledge of the identity of Jiva and Brahma, roots out all the fanciful distinctions of *I* and mine.

46. The perfect Atma-knowing Yogi, with his Gnyànic eye, sees the whole world as *existing in* himself and *as his* sole Atma-like self.

47. [How can you say that this world, which is plainly visible as an independent entity, is nothing different from Atma? The reply is as follows:—]

This whole world is Atma and nothing but Atma. As there are no vessels, &c., which are not made up of matter, so there is nothing wich is not Atma. Consequently, the *Gnyánee*, or one that possesses Gnyànam, sees or regards the whole world as his own self.

48. The shirking off of the pre-existing three Upádhis, viz., Sthúla, Súkshma, and Kàràna, and three attributes or *Gunams* viz., *Satwa*, *Rajasa*, and *Tamasa*, by an Atma-Gnyani, is said to be *Jivanmukti*. Such Gnyanee as is in this condition, with

the concomittants of Sat, Chit and Ananda, assumes the form of Brahma, as an insect—Kita—assumes the form of a fly—Bhramara.

49. Having tided over the great ocean of desire by the help of a ship—Gnyànam,— and killed giants—Love, Hatred, &c.,, —the Yogee is seen possessing the means of *Sama, Dama Uparati, Titiksha*, &c.. and fixing his Chittam on Atma.

50. The characteristic of a Jivanmukta is as follows :—

The Yogee, who is a Jivanmukta, having renounced all external pleasures as transient, and overwhelmed with the happiness of knowing and seeing and becoming (rather attaining) Atmaswarupa, always shines most brilliantly by self and unborrowed light as the light in a vessel or a globe.

51. [What kind of life must a Jivanmukta lead till *Karmic* effects are all exhausted ?]

Though he is a mere spectator in *Sthúla, Súkshma*, and *Karàna* Dehams or bodies, the Atmagnyáni or Jivanmukta must regard himself to be, like Akasa, intact with the attributes of *Sthulatwa, Sukshmatwa*, &c.; though he knows everything, he must be as an ignorant person; and he must not have a liking for the enjoyment of the undesired-for pleasures when such happen without his efforts. He must pass over all pleasures as smoothly and as unconcernedly as wind.

52. [Where is *Videha Kaivalyam* when Sthúla, Súkshma and Kàrana Dehams or bodies are all destroyed ?]

As water mixes with water, air with air, and fire with fire; so, after the three kinds of outer cloaks, viz., Sthúla, Súkshma ann Kàrana Sariras, are destroyed, the Gnyánee becomes most inseparably and indivisibly one with the all-pervading form of Brahma.

53. Who is Brahma ?

That something, than possessing which there is nothing more advantageous to be possessed, whose happiness or bliss is higher than the highest kind of happiness or bliss, and further than which nothing is to be known, is to be regarded as Brahma.

54. That something, after seeing which there is nothing more to be seen; after becoming which there is nothing more to become, or, in other words, there is no more rebirth; and after knowing which as oneself there is no more to be known —that something is Brahma.

55. That something, which fills everything brimful and crosswise, above and below; which is of the form of Sath, Chith, and Ananda; which is indivisible or has no second to it; which is endless; which is always present; and which is one and one alone;—that something is Brahma.

56. What is viewed by the Upanishads as everlasting, as the very form of perfect and undivided bliss, and as the unity; while non-Brahmic Dehàs, Indriyas, or senses, &c., are regarded as false and powerless—that is Brahma.

57. [It is said that Brahma, Vishnu, &c., possess perfect bliss. Then, why do not those, that perform sacrifices to obtain the *Lokams* or regions of Brahma, Vishnu, &c., become Brahma himself?]

It is replied that the bliss of Brahma, Vishnu, &c., is only a unit in the great whole of the perfect bliss of Atma. They —Brahma, Vishnu, &c.—possess a proportionately very small amount of bliss, and are proportionately very small beings.

58. [While it is palpable that every body loves the non-Atmic Deha, Indriyàs, &c., how can you assert that Atma alone is the object of our love?]

Since Atma pervades everything, and every deed or action, like ghee in milk, when we love anything or any work, we love, not the thing or work, but the underlying Atma in them both.

59. [Here below it is explained how to know that Atma is pervading everything and everywhere.]

What is neither thin nor thick, neither short nor long, neither lives nor dies, possesses neither form, attribute, caste, nor name, is Brahma or Atma.

60. What gives light to sun, moon, stars, &c., and what cannot be enlightened by sun, moon, &c., and what lightens all these shining objects, is Brahma.

61. Like a red-hot iron ball, Atma, pervading the whole world both inside and outside, enlightens it ; but, without being enlightened by anything else, shines with its own light.

62. Brahma is something distinct and different from the world ; yet there is nothing which is not Brahma. Like water in the mirage, the existence of the world, as distinct and different from Brahma, is a myth.

63. From the real wisdom, true knowledge, or *Tatwa-gnyana*, it is concluded that everything, that is seen and heard, is that Individual, Sath-Chith-Ananda Brahma Himself, and no other than Brahma.

64. [Why is not that Omnipresent Brahma visible alike to *Agnyana Chakshus* or Agnyanic eye as well as to *Gnyana Chakshus* ?]

An Atmagnyani alone can see the Omnipresent Sath-Chith-Ananda Atma ; while one, that believes in the fact that body, &c., are themselves Atma, cannot see the Omnipresent Atma, as a blind man cannot eye the brilliant sun.

65. The Jiva,—being purified of all kinds of filth which is the source of all *Sansara*, by the gnyanam acquired by means of *Sravana*, *Manana*, &c., as aforesaid,—shines like the burnt gold, with its inherent brilliancy.

66. Driving off the *Agnyanic* darkness and rising in the *Hrudakasa*, the all permeating, the all supporting Atma, like the Gnyanic Sun (Bodha Bhanu) shines and enlightens the whole world.

67. He, who has given up all kinds of observances, does not care for any side, any place, and any time ; and acquires that all-occuping, cold, &c.—killing eternally happy and eternally luminous *Swámtmatirtha* self-explaining (?) water—he becomes omnipresent and eternal, or, in brief, acquires omnipresence and eternity.

APPENDIX.

To the ATMABODHA

BY B. P. NARASIMMIAH B. A. F. T. S.

The marginal numbers in the Translation refer to the *Slokams* in the original.

12. The following table illustrates the process of the mixture of the elements forming Panchikaranam.

In it the letter E represents the undivided half of the Earth Element.

———	Ẃ	———	Water	———
———	F	———	Fire	———
———	W	———	Wind	———
———	A	———	A'kàsa or Ether	———

e represents the fourth part of the remaining half of the Earth Element.

———	ẇ	———	Water	———
———	f	———	Fire	———
———	w	———	Wind	———
———	a	———	A'kàsa	———

The following is the Mnemonic Table of Panchikaranam :—

A	aẇ	af	aw	ae
ẇa	Ẃ	ẃf	ẃw	ẃe
fa	fẇ	F	fw	fe
wa	wẇ	wf	W	we
ea	eẇ	ef	ew	E

A'tma is the 7th principle in man. (Vide Esoteric Buddhism, p. 21, on Atma, Manas, and Buddhi).

Antáhkaranam is the internal sense or sense of senses. [On several meanings of *Karanam, vide* Amaranighantu, 3rd Canto, 211 sloka.] The colloquial meaning of love, favour, &c., is vaguely and loosely applied to it; for true love or favour springs from the heart of hearts or internal heart and is not superficial.

Manas, Buddhi and Chittam. :—Though apparently these are one and the same, yet they are different from one another in their respective qualities. *Manas* is what is generally called Mind; but in reality is it only the doubting mind—while Buddhi is the determining Mind and *Chittam* is the unsteady and fickle mind. While *Manas* doubts and suspects everything, *Chittam* dwells only for a moment on an object and then passes on to another, and so on, but settles nowhere permanently, as listless birds fly from branch to branch and fly again. Buddhi plays the part of a judge. It settles the issues of doubting *Manas*. This is the result of deliberation.

Ahankaram :—(Vide Gurubàlaprabódhika, 1st Canto, Verse 204—Garvòbhimànóhankàró, &c. Here *Ahankára* is said to be that which causes the feeling of the superiority of self.) It is the sense or love of personality. Mr. Sinnett, in *Esoteric Buddhism,* (p. 83) says that "the student must bear in mind that *personality* is the synonym for limitation." This sentence perhaps, in other words,. means the limiting or confining everything to one's self or person, and finding nothing beyond to be attributed to, and thus narrowing the sphere of true apprehension and comprehension. This love of superiority of one's person is the source of much evil as we all know.

Samána Váyuvu :—Its seat is in the navel or thereabout. It digests food and distributes the digested portion to all parts of the system, and causes the being to live healthily.

Vyána Váyuvu :—Its seat is *in every part* of the body. Its function is to create perspiration, horripilation, &c.

Udána Váyuvu :—Its seat is in the neck or near the throat. It gives the power of talking. It brings up the sound.

Prána Váyuvu :—Its seat is in the chest. Its function is to cause respiration.

Apána Váyuvu :—Its seat is in the excretory organs. (Cf: Gudépanah. Amaranighantu, 1st Canto, 64th verse.) It expels matter and urine from the body.

For a more detailed explanation of this difficult subject of *Panchikaranam*, readers who understand Telugu are requested to refer to the Telugu *Sithárámánjanèyam* annotated by M. R. Ry. Pàlaparthi Nagèsvara Sasthrulu. Part II, verses 41-42, pp. 86-90.

14. *Ahamṣabdam* in this verse means *the sound of I, i. e.*, the remembrance of personality or self-love. *Jiva* is full of this quality from which *Atma* is free.

15. The five Kósams or the five coverings or coats are:—
Annamayakosam :—That physical body of flesh and blood which is born of food and semen, grows by food, and is bulky and composed of limbs.

Pranamayakósam :—It is made up of five *Karméndriyams* (*Vágìndriyam*, *Pánindriyam*, *Pádèndriyam*, *Páyrindriyam* and *Oopasténdriyam*), and five Prànams (*Prána*, *Apána*, *Vyána*, *Udána* and *Sámana*). *Vide* (the last and 2nd columns, from above, in the Table of *Pánchikaranam* given in the Translation of the 12th Slókam.)

Manòmayakòsam :—Is made up of manas (doubting mind), Chittam (unsteady mind), and five *Gnyanèndriyams*—*Thwak*, *Chakshus*, *Sròtra*, *Jihva*, and *Aghrána*—Skin, Eyes, Ears, Tongue and Nose, respectively, for the explanation of which terms read the 3rd column from above in the table of *Panchikaranam* in the 12th Slókam, horizontally.)

Vignyánamayakòsam :—Is composed of *Buddhi* (determining mind and *Sabda* (Sound), *Sparsa* (Touch), *Rùpa* (Form), *Rasa* (Taste), and *Gandha* (Smell.)

A'nandamayakósam :—That *Agnyánam* itself which is composed of eternal love and delight, and their functions which are the chief cause of the origin of this world.

16. *S'ravana* :—Hearing or listening to the meaning of *Védás*, &c.

Mananu :—Thinking over such meanings and trying to reconcile the seeming inconsistencies, and to find out the real meaning of the *Védas* and then to begin to actively meditate upon such real meaning.

Nididhyásana :—This meditation is used to enable one to give up the unnatural qualities, viz., Lust, Hatred, Miserliness, Vanity, Revenge, Blind Desire; and to acquire that resolute belief in the identification of oneself with Brahma.

18. (Vide the table of *Panchikaranam*, 12th Slókam. Read 1st column from above horizontally and refer to the Appendix on it.)

19. *Indriyavishayamúla* :—The objects of *Indriyams* or senses..

20. *Satchidánanda A'tma* :—*Sat* (*Satya*=true, eternal)+Chith (*Gnyána* or omniscience adj: omniscient) + A'nanda (Delight or Bliss. Perfect Bliss.) A'tma who is Eternal, Omniscient, and perfectly Blissful.

23. *Sat, Chita, A'nanda, Nitya, Nirmalatva. Sat*: that which is undestroyed in wakeful hours, dream, and sleep. *Chit*: *Gnyanam* or divine knowledge. *A'nanda*: eternal bliss. *Nitya*: that which is existing always. *Nirmalatva*: the purity and serenity of form and body.

29. *Kinchidgnyatwa* :—Knowing a little or something.

Sarvagnyatwa :—Knowing much or everything.

31. *Asti, Jáyaté, Vardhaté, Parinamate, Apakshiyaté*, and *Vinasyati*. *Asti*=To be or exist. *Jáyaté*=To be born. *Vardhaté*=To grow. *Parinamaté* = To ripen. *Apakshiyaté*=To decay. *Vinasyati*=To die.

86. *Avarandsakti* is that power which causes one to forget that knowledge of oneself though one is seeing one's own self: and, absorbing the difference between oneself and another, originates that difference again—e. g. sleep.

Vikshepásakti :—Is that power which causes the knowledge of difference in *Jágrat* and *Swapnávasthas*, i. e., in wakeful and dreaming hours.

40. *Thriputi* is the Sanskrit word for *Gnyatru* (the knower or one that knows), *Gnyana* (knowing) and *Gnéya* (that which is known.)

41. *Dhyánam* is no other process than active contemplation or meditation of Theosophists.

Antahkaranam is that internal sense whose purity, firmness and work are more to be cared for, and on whose adopting the right course and on whose success in that line depends one's spiritual development.

Gnyánam is the knowledge, the spiritual or divine knowledge, which is the result of the work of *Antahkaranam* working in right direction.

Agnyanam is the antithesis of the aforesaid *Gnyanam.*

48. *Satwagunams* :—Spiritually best qualities.

Rájasagunams :—Materially or worldly good qualities.

Támasagunams :—Worldly worst qualities.

Jivanmukta :—Literally means one who has given up *Jiva* or life; but really one who is *in* this world though not *of* it.

49. The fact of an insect assuming the form of a fly is known in Sanskrit as *Bhramarakitanyayam.* This law is known to every school boy in India and abroad. Hindoo boys have very often tried this experiment and succeeded. The process is simple. Make a paper box or a tube; put a bee and a green caterpillar with some tender leaves in the box; and close the box. Then the bee begins its operation. It sits to look steadily into the face of the insect; whenever the latter moves a little, the bee stings it. This punitory discipline

continued for a week or so, creates such terror and fright in the insect that it entirely forgets everything, nay its self-existence, but the form of its terrible master—bee; till by the end of nearly a fortnight the insect gradually assumes through this dreadful active meditation and devotion the very form of the bee with wings; and flies off as a bee when the lid is opened. This is both practically and scientifically true. This explains also the law of Affinity or Molecular attraction or Integration of homogeneous particles and the molecular repulsion or disintegration of heterogeneous ones.

49. *S'ama, Dama,* &c. Referring the reader to the article on the *Qualifications for Chelaship* in the September 1884 *Theosophist* in the opening page, for a better explanation of these terms, I shall here add my own explanation of the same with the view of assisting those readers that cannot conveniently see the article referred to.

(1) *S'ama* is controlling or overcoming the internal sense or passion.

(2) *Dama* is curbing the external senses or passion.

(3) *Uparati* is gradually giving up the observance of all rituals and ceremonies as the acquisition of divine knowledge increases. This is the true meaning of *Sannyasam* or asceticism.

(4) *Titikshá* is being unaffected by heat and cold, joy and sorrow.

(5) *S'radhdhá* is loving the Guru, the Ruler of the universe, the *Vedas* and *Sástras.*

(6) *Samádhána* is enjoying the tranquillity of mind after finding the satisfactory explanations of the doubtful and intricate points or *Mahávakyams* inculcated by the Guru;—rather tranquilising one's own mind after finding one's Guru's teachings corroborated by the explanations given in *Sástras.*

52. *Vidèhakaivalyam:*—a man is called a *Jiivanmukta,* whose sole profession is the acquisition of *Gnyánam.* This *Jivanmukta* gives no room for *Agámi* and *Sanchit* karmams, for he

neither is doing nor does any action whose consequence will be in store for his enjoyment; but he is still subject to consequential results of his past actions or actions of his past life. He *must* taste their fruits whether sweet or sour. This is what is called *Prárabdha* which exhausts in its enjoyment. Thus he the *Jívanmukta,* suffers fully in his *Sthúla S'arira* which dies the moment the *Prarabdha* karma is exhausted. He dies now once for all, and attains the *Kaivalyam* or *Moksham* from which he never returns and therfore has no more rebirth, and which therefore is called *Vidèhakaivalyam* or literally *body-less-nirvana.*

57. *Brahma, Vishnu, Siva,* &c. Here *Brahma* is the creating principle. The *S'astras* personify the same, give it a body, and say that it is the embodiment of *Satvaguna.*

66. *Hridákasa,* i. e., the *A'kasa* or sky of *Hridaya* or heart. This is a figurative word. As the sun rises in the sky, so *Gnyánam,* which is compared to the sun, rises in the *Hridaya* or heart which again is compared to the sky.

॥ श्रीवाक्यसुधा ॥

SHRÍ-VAKYASUDHÁ

TRANSLATED WITH NOTES

BY

MANILAL N. DVIVEDI, F. T. S.

रूपं दृश्यं लोचनं दृग् दृग् दृश्यं दृक् तु मानसम् ।
दृश्या धीवृत्तयःसाक्षी दृगेव न तु दृश्यते ॥ १ ॥

FORM is the object, and the eye is the subject of all our objective perception; the eye, however, is cognised by the mind, (the phenomena of) which again are objects of perception to the ever present subjective *A'tman* (spirit), which in the series can never be the object of any ultimate perception.*

नीलपीतस्थूलसूक्ष्म ह्रस्वदीर्घादिभेदतः ।
नानाविधानि रूपाणि पश्येल्लोचनमेकधा ॥ २ ॥

The eye, perceiving various forms, such as blue, yellow, large, small, short, long, etc., remains all the same—ever unaffected and uniformly one. [The rule of perception, implied is this: those are *objects* of perception (दृश्य), which possess the property of presenting themselves in *many* forms; and those are *subjects*

---

* Compare.

कर्त्तारं च क्रियां तद्वद् व्यावृत्तविषयानपि ।
स्फोरयेदेकयत्नेन योऽसौसाक्ष्यत्रचिद्वपुः ॥
ईक्षे शृणोमि जिघ्रामि स्वादयामि स्पृशाम्यहं ।
इति भासयते सर्वं नृत्यशालास्थदीपवत् ॥

पंचदशी ॥ १० ॥ ९ ॥ १० ॥

"Antaskarna is the path of communion between soul and body, entirely disconnected with the former; existing with, belonging to, and dying with the body."—*Editor's note Theosophist, Vol. IV, No. 11, p. 268.*

or perception (द्रष्ट), with regard to any the same perception which remain *one and unaffected* by the forms of the objects cognised.]

आंध्यमांद्यपटुत्वेषु नेत्रधर्मेषु चैकधा ।
संकल्पयेन्मनःश्रोत्रत्वगादौ योज्यतामिदम् ॥ ३ ॥

The keenness, slowness, or blindness of sight imply various properties in the eye, (present the eye under *many forms*), all cognised by the mind, which remains *one and unaffected*. The same may, by parity of reasoning, be said of the other organs of sense, as the ear, the skin, &c.

कामसंकल्पसंदेहाः श्रद्धाऽश्रद्धेधृतीतरे ।
ह्रीर्धीर्भीरित्येवमादीन् भासयत्येकधा चितिः ॥ ४ ॥

The mind again is an *object* of perception : the *A'tman* cognises the whole phenomena of the mind, viz., desire, imagination, doubt, belief, disbelief shame, intelligence, fear, etc.; remaining itself unique and unaffected.

(The *A'tman* cannot be assumed to be the *object* of any further perception; for such a theory would involve us in confusion *ad-infinitum*. Nor is the absurdity that the *A'tman* itself is both the *subject and object* of perception at all tenable. The *Atman* therefore shines by its own lustre and illumines all other objects of perception.)

नोदेति नास्तमेत्येषो न वृद्धिं याति न क्षयम् ।
स्वयं विभात्यथाऽन्यानि भासयेत् साधनं विना ॥ ५ ॥

The *(A'tman)* never appears or disappears, never waxes or wanes. It shines by its own light and enlightens the whole without any (exterior) help.

The substance implied is this: that, which does not shine by its own light, is subject to transformation, as *Ahankára* (egoism). Again, *A'tman* enlightens the whole as साक्षी-द्रष्टा and is therefore not subject to change; for that, which does not shine *independently* of *visible matter* (जड), is not free from change (निर्विकार) as *egoism*, etc. Thus *Atman*, being beyond all change (निर्विकार) and shining by its own lustre (स्वंयप्रकाश), ever remains the *subject* (द्रष्टा) of all knowledge. and can never be *object* of any ultimate perception. This subjective *A'tman* is thus proved to be *Paramatman*. It is the one implied by त्वम् in the *Sruti* तत्त्वमसि ; and is one with the परब्रह्म implied by तत् in the same. Though in this manner *A'tman* and *Paramátman* are one and the same, it is necessary to dispel the *ignorance* which interferes with the realisation of their unity.

The Linga Deha.

चिच्छायावेशतो बुद्धौ भानं धीस्तु द्विधा स्थिता ।
एकाऽहंकृतिरन्या स्यादन्तःकरणरूपिणी ॥ ६ ॥

A reflection of the *A'tman* in *Buddhi* enkindles it (makes the substantially *material Buddhi* believe itself to be entire *spirit*). This *Buddhi* is of two sorts: *Ahankára* and *Antaskarana*. (The *doer* the *subject* of all action is *Ahankára*; and the *Antaskarana* or *Manas* is its instrument.)*

छायाऽहंकारयो रैक्यं तप्तायःपिण्डवन्मतम् ।
तदहंकारतादात्म्याद्देहश्चेतनतामियात् ॥ ७ ॥

The unity of *Ahankára* with the reflection of *A'tman* is as inseparable as that of a heated ball of iron with the fire that heats it. *Ahankára* identifies itself with the external physical body also, which thereupon becomes spiritualized: believes itself to be all spirit.†

---

* Compare.

अहंमित्यभिमंता यः कर्ता ऽसौतस्य साधनं ।
मनस्तस्य क्रिये त ऽर्बहिर्वृत्तक्रिमोरिथते ॥
अंतर्मुखहमित्येषा वृत्तिःकर्तारमुल्लिखेत् ।
बहिर्मुखेदमित्येषा बाह्यं वस्त्विदमुल्लिखेत. ॥
पंचदशी ॥ १० ॥ ६ ॥ ७ ॥

† Compare.

अहं वृत्तौ चिदाभासः कामक्रोधादिकेषु च
संव्याप्य वर्तते तप्ते लोहे वन्हि यथा तथा ॥ पंचदशी ॥ ८ ॥ १८ ॥

अहंकारस्य तादात्म्यं चिच्छायादेहसाक्षिभिः ।
सहजं कर्मजं भ्रांतिजन्यं च त्रिविधं क्रमात् ॥ ८ ॥

The indentification of *Ahankára* with the reflection of *A'tman*, with the physical external shell, and with the *subject* of all knowledge—*A'tman,*—is respectively *inherent* (is from the beginning of *Ahankára*) through *actions* (*i. e.*, कर्म, as those performed during the waking state), and through *ignorance* (अविद्या).

संबंधिनः सतो नास्ति निवृत्तिः सहजस्य तु ।
कर्मक्षयात्प्रबोधाच्च निवर्तेत क्रमादुभे ॥ ९ ॥

Of these three, the inherent identification of *Ahankára* with the reflection of *A'tman* is never destroyed; whereas; that with the other two is destroyed by the exhaustion of कर्म, and by knowledge respectively.

अहंकारलये सुप्तो भवेद्देहोप्यचेतनः ।
अहंकृतिविकासोऽर्धः स्वप्नःपूर्णस्तु जागरः ॥१०॥

When *Ahankára* merges into original ignorance, sleep is induced, and the physical body (स्थूलदेह), which appeared with spirit by its identification with *Ahankára* in the waking state, becomes as it were lifeless. *Ahankára* is half awake, the state produced in the astral body (लिंगदेह) is the one called dream; and when it is wide awake, the state produced is sleeplessness or waking. (Thus all कर्म is dependent on *Ahankára* which when quite absent as in sleep, gives rise to none.)*

---

* "The Vedantic philosophy teaches as much as Occult philosophy that our *Monad*, during its life on earth as a triad (7th, 6th, and 5th principles), has, besides the condition of pure intelligence, three conditions; viz., waking, dreaming and *sushupti*—a state of dreamless sleep—from the stand-point of terrestrial conception; of real actual soul-life from the occult stand-point. While man is either dreamlessly profoundly asleep or in a trance-state, the triad (spirit soul and the mind) enters into perfect union with the *paramtaman* —the Supreme universal soul" :—*Editor's Note Theosophist, Vol. IV., No. 11, p. 267.*

क्रमाद्विच्छिद्य विच्छिद्य जायन्ते वृत्तयोऽखिलाः ।
सर्वा अपि विलीयंते सुप्तिमूर्छासमाधिषु ॥
पंचदशी ॥ ८ ॥ २० ॥

अन्तःकरणवृत्तिश्च चिच्छायैक्यमुपागता ।
वासना कल्पयेत् स्वप्ने बोधे च विषयान् वहिः ॥११॥

The *Antaskarana*, identifying itself with the reflection of *Atman*, creates, in dream, the impressions (वासना) necessary for the action of such कर्म as affect the astral body (सूक्ष्मदेह) and, in the waking state, the *objective* realities (our interest in those realities) necessary for the enjoyment of such कर्म as affect the physical form (स्थूलदेह).

मनोऽहंकृत्युपादानं लिङ्गमेकं जडात्मकम् ।
अवस्थात्रयमन्वेति जायते म्रियते तथा ॥१२॥

The astral body *(Linga deha)*, which is made up of *Manas* and *Ahankára*, is essentially material in its nature. It experiences the three states of waking, dreaming and sleeping, as undergoes also the transformations of death and birth.*

Máyá and its powers.

शक्तिद्वयं हि मायाया विक्षेपावृत्तिरूपकम् ।
विक्षेपशक्ति लिङ्गादि ब्रह्माण्डान्तं जगत्सृजेत् ॥१३॥

Having described how लिंगदेह is the basis of all our ordinary intercourse, it is proposed to examine the genesis of this देह from *Maya* or illusion. *Máya* has two powers. *Vikshepa* and *Avarana*, of which *Vikshepa* or *ext‹nsion* evolves the whole world, beginning from the लिंगदेह to the all-embracing universe, from *Brahma*.

सृष्टिर्नामब्रह्मरूपे सच्चिदानन्दवस्तुनि ।
अब्धौ फेनादिवत् सर्वं नामरूपप्रसारणम् ॥१४॥

This evolution may be described as the attributing name and form to that *Brahma* which is all existence, all knowledge, and all joy—like the attributing of name and form as फेन (foam) तरंग (waves), बुद्बुद (bubbles), &c., to the waters of the ocean.

---

* Compare.

शोकहर्षभयक्रोध लोभमोहस्पृहादयः ।
अहंकारस्य दृश्यन्ते जन्ममृत्युश्च नात्मनः ॥ भगवद्गीता ॥

अन्तर्दृग्दृश्ययोर्भेदं बहिश्च ब्रह्मसर्गयोः ।
आवृणोत्यपरा शक्तिः सा संसारस्य कारणम् ॥१५॥

That is another power of *Máya-Avarana* or *immersion*—which, as the cause of this world, throws, as it were, the veil of reality over the unreal internal distinction between the object and the subject of knowledge, as also over the external one between *Brahma* and creation.

साक्षिणः पुरतो भातं लिङ्गदेहेन संयुतम् ।
चितिच्छायासमावेशा ज्जीवः स्याद् व्यावहारिकः॥१६॥

That लिंगशरीर, which shines by the reflection of the immovable *Átman*, the witness of all phenomena and noumena, and which is, as it were, one with the स्थूलशरीर, the external shell, becomes (by the force of *Avarana Sakti*) जीव in our ordinary life *i. e.*, is for our ordinary intercourse termed जीव or soul.

अस्य जीवत्वमारोपात् साक्षिण्यप्यवभासते ।
आवृतौ तु विनष्टायां भेदे भातेऽपयाति तत् ॥१७॥

By the force of the same *Avarana*, the witness of all the कूटस्थब्रह्म also shines as if it were जीव. The आवरण being destroyed by (ज्ञान), this illusion melts away.

तथा सर्गब्रह्मणोश्च भेदमावृत्य तिष्ठति ।
या शक्ति स्तद्वशाद् ब्रह्म विकृतत्वेन भासते ॥१८॥

Similarly *Brahma* appears manipulated into many forms by the force of that power *(Avarana)* which covers the distinction (unreal distinction) between creation and *Brahma*.

अत्राऽप्यावृत्तिनाशेन विभाति ब्रह्मसर्गयो ।
भेदस्तयो र्विकारः स्यात्सर्गे न ब्रह्मणि क्वचित् ॥१९॥

Here also, by the destruction of *Avarana*, the distinction between *Brahma* and creation becomes so far clear, as to enable us to attribute all change (विकार), viz., name and form; to the latter and not to the former.

अस्ति भाति प्रियं रूपं नाम चेत्यंशपञ्चकम् ।
आद्यं त्रयं ब्रह्मरूपं जगद्रूपं ततो द्वयम् ॥२०॥

All intercourse implies five attributes and no more: existence (सत्); intelligence (चित्); love (आनंद); form (रूप); and name (नाम). The first three of these represent the all-pervading *Brahma*, and the last two the unreal *Jagat* (world creation).

खंवाय्वग्निजलोर्वीषु देवतिर्यङ्नरादिषु ।
अभिन्नसच्चिदानन्दा भिद्येते रूपनामनी ॥२१॥

In the elements, *Akása*, *Váyu*, *Tejas*, *Apas*, and *Prithvi*; as also in the different degrees of creation, gods, birds, animals and men;—the *Sat*, *Chit* and *Ananda*, are ever one and uniform—that which differs is simply the form and the name.

The course of realising Brahma Tatva
(Samádhi or concentration.)

उपेक्ष्य नामरूपे द्वे सच्चिदानन्दतत्परः ।
समाधिं सर्वदा कुर्या द्धृदये चाथवा बहिः ॥२२॥

Neglecting therefore the unreal creation consisting of mere name and form (abstracting all one's interest from the objects of this world), one (desirous of final absolution) should meditate on the *Satchidanand Brahma*, and should ever practise mental as well as physical concentration.

सविकल्पो निर्विकल्पः समाधि र्द्विविधो हृदि ।
दृश्यशब्दानुवेधेन सविकल्पः पुन र्द्विधा ॥२३॥

Mental concentration is of two kinds:—*Savikalpaka* and *Nirvikalpaka*; the former again is of two kinds: *Drishyanuviddha* and *Shabdanuviddha*.

कामाद्या श्चित्तगा दृश्या स्तत्साक्षित्वेन चेतनम् ।
ध्यायेद् दृश्यानुविद्धोऽयं समाधिः सविकल्पकः ॥२४॥

The दृश्यानुविद्धसविकल्पसमाधि is the meditation upon the subjective *Atman*, as the witness of the mental world—the passions, desires, &c., arising in the *Manas*.

असङ्गःसच्चिदानन्दः स्वप्रभो द्वैतवर्जितः ।
अस्मीतिशब्दविद्धोऽयं समाधिः सविकल्पकः ॥२५॥

The शब्दानुविद्धसविकल्पसमाधि is the fixing one's mind on "I am (that) *Brahma*" which is (described in the Vedás) as self-existent eternal all-intelligence and love, self-illumined and unique in itself

स्वानुभूतिरसावेशाद् दृश्यशब्दानुपेक्षते ।
निर्विकल्पसमाधिः स्यान्निर्वातस्थितदीपवत् ॥२६॥

That is *Nirvikalpa Samadhi* in which, through the ecstacy, of the pleasure consequent upon the knowledge of one's self the *mental* (दृश्य) as well as *the nominal* (शब्द) are both overlooked; and (the mind) stands like the jet of a lamp burning in a place protected from the slightest breeze.*

हृदीव बाह्यदेशेऽपि यस्मिन् कस्मिंश्च वस्तुनि ।
समाधिराद्यः सन्मात्रान्नामरूपपृथक्कृतिः ॥२७॥

The separation in any external object of sight, of name and form, from its original *substratum*, *sat* is *external, phenomenal* (दृश्यानुविद्ध) concentration (like the *internal mental* one described before).

अखण्डैकरसं वस्तु सच्चिदानन्दलक्षणम् ।
इत्यविच्छिन्नचिन्तेयं समाधिर्मध्यमो भवेत् ॥२८॥

The meditation on the one, unique, and *Satchidánanda Brahma* (described in the S'ruties), as the only reality in this universe is *external, nominal* (शब्दानुविद्ध) concentration.

---

* Compare.

यथा दीपो निवातस्थो नेङ्गते सोपमा स्मृता ।
योगिनो यतचित्तस्य युञ्जतो योगमात्मनः ॥

भगवद्गीता ॥ ६ ॥ १९ ॥

स्तब्धीभावो रसास्वाद स्तृतीयः पूर्ववन्मतः ।
एतैः समाधिभिः षड्भि र्नयेत् कालं निरन्तरं ॥२९॥

The third (*Nirvikalpa Samádhi*) concentration is like the one described before, cessation of all thought except the enjoyment of the one eternal pleasure arising from the experience of the universal *Paramátman* (which thus proves to be one with the subjective *Atman* shown as the subject of *internal Nirvikalpa Samádhi*). Every one should devote the whole of his time to these six kinds of *Samadhis.*

देहाभिमाने गलिते विज्ञाते परमात्मनि ।
यत्र यत्र मनोयाति तत्र तत्र समाधयः ॥३०॥

The egoism in the physical body being annihilated in this manner, and *Universal Atman* being thoroughly realised, wherever the mind of the ascetic is directed, there it *naturally* loses itself into one or other of these *Samádhis.*

भिद्यते हृदयग्रन्थिश्छिद्यन्ते सर्वसंशयाः ।
क्षीयन्ते चास्यकर्माणि तस्मिन् दृष्टे परावरे ॥३१॥ *

The identification of the phenomenal as well as the noumenal with the one eternal unchangeable *Brahma* being realised, the knot (of the unreal identification of *Ahankára* with *Atman* of the heart is at once split open; all doubts vanish in a minute; and all *Karma* (*Sanchita, Prárabdha,* and *Kriyámana*) is destroyed in the very bud. [*Karma* does not affect the absolved ascetic. *Prárabdha* or that part of *Sanchita,* of which this life is an evolute, runs its course and ends with this life; *Kriyámana* or that, which is being done at present in obedience to *Prárabdha,* has no stability in as much as its

---

* This S'ruti is taken from the Mandukya Upanishad, with which compare.

यदा सर्वे प्रभिद्यन्ते हृदयग्रंथयास्त्विाति ।
कामा ग्रंथिस्वरूपेण व्याख्याता वाक्यशेषतः ॥

पंचदशी ॥ ६ ॥ २६० ॥

store-house is destroyed by the destruction of *Lingadeha*; and *Sanchita*, (or that portion of past *Karma*, which has not yet borne fruit, plus the results of present *Karma* which are to bear their fruit) also has no room for its operation; for the *Lingadeha*, through which all its future manifestations on the plat-form of our physical frame become possible, has no existence.*]

The unity of Atman and Parmátman or Brahma.

अवच्छिन्न श्चिदाभास स्तृतीयः स्वप्नकल्पितः ।
विज्ञेय स्त्रि विधो जीव स्तत्राद्यः पारमार्थिकः ॥३२॥

Jiva is of three kinds: the first is that portion of *Brahma*, which is limited (by *Avidyá* and *Ahankára*); the second is the reflection of the *Atman* into the *Lingadeha*); and the third is the one imagined as active in dreams. Of these three, it is the first only which has any real existence. (If जीव is only a limited portion of *Brahma*, how can it be *Brahma* itself? With this doubt in view, it is said):—

अवच्छेदः कल्पितः स्यादवछेद्यं तु वास्तवं ।
तस्मिन् जीवत्वमारोपाद् ब्रह्मत्वं तु स्वभावतः ॥३३॥

The limit (in *Brahma*) is simply imaginary (since it is destructible by the merging of *Ahankára* and *Avidyá* into *Brahma* by proper knowledge) and the *real thing* is that which is limited (viz., *Brahma*). It is assumed to be *Jiva* only by imagination, but by nature it is (one with) *Brahma*.

---

* Compare.

ज्ञानाग्निः सर्वकर्माणि भस्मसात्कुरुतेऽर्जुन ॥ भगवद्गीता ॥

also आत्मानं चेद्विजानीया दयमस्मीति पूरुषः ।
किमिच्छन् कस्य कामाय शरीरमनुसंज्वरेत् ॥
पंचदशी ॥ ७ ॥ १ ॥

also न निरोधो न चोत्पत्तिर्न बद्धो न च साधकः ।
न मुमुक्षुर्न वै मुक्त इत्येषा परमार्थता ॥ पंचदशी ॥ ८ ॥ ७१ ॥

अवच्छिन्नस्य जीवस्य पूर्णेन ब्रह्मणैक्यता ।
तत्वमस्यादिवाक्येन जगुर्नेतरजीवयोः ॥ ३४ ॥

It is the unity of this imaginary *Jíva* with *Brahma*, that is inculcated in such phrases as तत्त्वमसि (in the *Chhándogya Upanishad*); and not with the other *Jíva*.*

ब्रह्मण्यवस्थिता माया विक्षेपावृत्तिरूपिणी ।
आवृत्याखण्डतां तस्मिन् जगज्जीवे प्रकल्पयेत् ॥३५॥

In *Brahma* exists *Máya* in its two aspects of विक्षेप and आवृत्ति, which, covering the unique, unchangeable *Brahma*, attributes the universe and the soul to it (evolves the universe from it.)

जीवोधिस्थचिदाभासो भवेद्भोक्ता हि कर्मकृत् ।
भोग्यरूपमिदं सर्वं जगत् स्याद्भूतभौतिकम् ॥३६॥

The reflection of *Atman* in *Buddhi* is the *Jíva* which enjoys the fruits of its *Karma*; and this transitory universe is the thing that is enjoyed by it.

अनादिकालमारभ्य मोक्षात् पूर्वमिदं द्वयम् ।
व्यवहारे स्थितं तस्मादुभयं व्यावहारिकम् ॥३७॥

The duality (of *Jíva* and *Jagat* which exists from time immemorial† has any reality only till the time‡ of final absolution. It is therefore useful only so far as our ordinary intercourse is concerned.

---

* Compare.—

एकमेवाद्वितीयं सन्नाम रूपविवर्जितम् ।
सृष्टेः पुराऽधुनाप्यस्य तादृक्त्वं तदि इतीर्यते ॥
श्रोतुर्देहेन्द्रियातीतं वस्त्वत्रत्वपदेरितम् ।
एकता ग्राह्यतेऽसीति तदैक्यमनुभूयताम् ॥
पंचदशी ॥ ६ ॥ ७ ॥ ८ ॥

† Compare.—

प्रकृतिं पुरुषं चैव विद्ध्यनादी उभावपि ॥ भगवद्गीता ॥

‡ Compare.—

चोद्यं वा परिहारो वा क्रियतां द्वैतभाषया ।
अद्वैतभाषया चोद्यं नास्ति ॥ पंचदशी ॥

(This duality is of two kinds: ईश्वरकृत and जीवकृत; the destruction of the latter is necessary for absolution;* for the name and form given to the objects of this world is a creation, purely mental and obstructive to absolution, as such.)†

चिदा भासस्थिता निद्रा विक्षेपावृत्तिरूपिणी ।
आवृत्यजीवजगती पूर्वे नूत्ने तु कल्पयेत् ॥२८॥

The sleep, which, in its two aspects of *Vikshepa* and *Avarana*, is the quality of reflected *A'tman*, covers the whole of *Jiva* and *Jagat* (in sleep) and creates (in dreams) new ones in their place.

These are called the प्रातिभासिक *Jiva* and *Jagat*. The comparison implied is this:—Just as sleep resides in the चिदाभास, *Máya* resides, as it were, potentially in ब्रह्म; and, as sleep covers the व्यावहारिकजीव and जगत् and creates the प्रातिभासिक ones in their place, so *Máya* covers ब्रह्म and evolves from it the व्यावहारिक जीव and जगत् instead.)

प्रतीतिकाल एवैते स्थितत्वात् प्रातिभासिके ।
नहि स्वप्नप्रबुद्धस्य पुनः स्वप्नस्थितिस्तयोः ॥२९॥

As these (*Jiva Jagat*) appear real only during the time of their existence, (*i. e.* in dream) they are called प्रातिभासिक or imaginary: they are never felt in any other dream after one is awakened from the original dream in which they were experienced.

---

* Compare.

अतः सर्वस्य जीवस्य बंधकृन्मानसं जगत् ॥ पंचदशी ॥ ४ ॥ ३५ ॥
जीवन्मुक्ते पराकाष्ठा जीवद्वैतविवर्जनात् ।
लभ्यतेऽसावतोऽत्रेदमीशद्वैताद्विवेचितम् ॥ पंचदशी ॥ ४ ॥ ६१ ॥

† Compare.

मूषासिक्तं यथाताम्रं तन्निभं जायते तथा ।
रूपादीन्व्याप्नुवच्चित्तं तन्निभंदृश्यतेध्रुवम् ॥
सर्वार्थव्यंजकत्वाध्वी र्थाकाराप्रदृश्यते ।
पंचदशी ॥ ४ ॥ २८ ॥ २९ ॥

(The previous illustration is thus carried to its legitimate and logical result. As the प्रातिभासिक जीव and जगत् are real only till the dream is broken, so also are व्यावहारिक जीव and जगत् real only till the spell of *Máya* is broken by ज्ञान; and also as the व्यावहारिक is one and unchangeable in the प्रातिभासिक creation, so is परब्रह्म in the व्यावहारिक creation. Thus the proposition enunciated in verse 37 is established.)

प्रातिभासिकजीवो यस्तज्जगत् प्रातिभासिकम् ।
वास्तवं मन्यतेऽन्यस्तु मिथ्येति व्यावहारिकः ॥४०॥

The प्रातिभासिक जीव believes the प्रातिभासिक जगत् to be real; whereas the व्यावहारिक जीव knows both of them to be false.

व्यावहारिकजीवो य स्तज्जगद् व्यावहारिकम् ।
सत्यं प्रत्येति मिथ्येति मन्यते पारमार्थिकः ॥४१॥

So does the व्यावहारिक जीव believe the व्यावहारिक जगत् to be real; but the परमार्थिकजीव (ब्रह्म) knows both of them to be false. (This व्यावहारिक जगत् exists only so long as व्यावहारिक जीव exists. Both are therefore unreal to the पारमार्थिक जीव. In sleep, as also at the time of *Pralaya*, both these disappear, *Brahma* alone sustaining; so also in those who are जीवन्मुक्त, absolved even while living.)

पारमार्थिकजीवस्तु ब्रह्मैक्यं पारमार्थिकम् ।
प्रत्येति वीक्षते नान्य द्वीक्षते त्वनृतात्मताम् ॥४२॥

The *Páramárthika Jiva* knows itself to be one with *Brahma*, and sees nothing apart from it except perhaps the unreality of every thing besides it.

माधुर्यद्रवशैत्यादि जलधर्मा स्तरङ्गके ।
अनुगम्याथ तन्निष्ठे फेनेऽप्यनुगता यथा ॥४३॥

As sweetness, fluidity, coolness and other qualities of water, are found in the waves that surge on its bosom, and also in the foam that plays on the surface of waves:

k

साक्षिस्थाः सच्चिदानन्दाः संबन्धाद् व्यावहारिके ।
तद्द्वारेणानुगच्छन्ति तथैव प्रातिभासिके ॥४४॥

So do the सत्, चित् and आनंद—, which are inherent in the परमात्मन्, the witness of all—appear in the व्यावहारिक जगत् and, through it, in the प्रातिभासिक जगत् also. (Vide verse No. 20.)

लये फेनस्य तद्धर्मा द्रवाद्या स्युस्तरङ्गके ।
तस्यापि विलये नीरे तिष्ठन्त्येते यथा पुरा ॥४५॥

On the disappearance of foam, its qualities fluidity, &c., merge into its source, the wave; and, on the disappearance of the latter, its qualities again merge into its source, water, and remain there as before.

प्रातिभासिकजीवस्य लये स्युर्व्यावहारिके ।
तल्लये सच्चिदानन्दाः पर्यवस्यन्ति साक्षिणि ॥४६॥

So, on the disappearance of the *imaginary* जीव its constituents (सत्, चित्, आनंद) flow into its source, the *ordinary* जीव, on whose disappearance again all these—the residuum—flow into the source whence everything emanated—the परमात्मन्, Universal Spirit—witness af all.*

॥ इति ब्रह्मार्पणमस्तु. ॥

---

* Compare.

यद्यद् रूपादि कल्पेत बुध्यातत्तत् प्रकाशयन ।
तस्यतस्य भवेत्साक्षि स्वतो वाग्बुध्यगोचरः ॥
कथंताहङनवाम्राह्य इति चेन्मैव गृह्यतां ।
सर्वं ग्रहोपसंशांतौ स्वयमेवावशिष्यते ॥ पंचदशी ॥ २३ ॥ २४ ॥

VEDÁNT SÁRA.[a]

OF

SADÁNANDA SWÁMI

Translated by MR. W. WARD.

Véda-vyása obtained, by religious austerities, the discourse which Krishna held with Arjoona, and, for the following reasons, from this discourse wrote the védánta: To humble Kákutst'ha, a king of the race of the sun, who was intoxicated with an idea of his own wisdom: To point out, that the knowledge of Bramha, is the only certain way of obtaining liberation, instead of the severe mortifications of former yugas, which mankind at present are incapable of performing, and to destroy among men attachment to works of merit; since, so long as the desire of reward remaineth, men can never be delivered from liability to future birth. Shankaráchárya wrote a comment on the Védánta, and a disciple of Adwaita-nanda-parama-hangsa, a Sanyasi, composed, from this comment, the Védánta-Sára.

After this introduction, the author proceeds: The meaning of Vèdánta is, the last part of the Véda; or the "gnana kanda" which is also an Upanishad.

He who, knowing the contents of the Véda, and of the Angas,[b] is free from the desire of reward as the fruit of his actions; from the guilt of the murder of Bràmhans, cows, women, and children; from the crime of adultery; who performs the duties of the Shástra and of his caste, cherishing his relations, &c; who practises the ceremonies which follow the birth of a son, &c.; offers the appointed atonements; observes fasts; bestows alms; who continues, according to the directions of the Véda, absorbed in meditation on Bramha, and believes, that, seeing every thing proceeded from Bramha, and that, at

---

a. From Véda, and anta the end.—*Sára* means essence, and therefore the title of this work imports, that it is the essence of the Védânta philosophy.

b. Branches or members of the Véda.

the destruction of the universe (as earthen vessels of every description, when broken, return to the clay from whence they were formed), all things will be absorbed in him again and that therefore Bramha is every thing, is heir to the Véda.

All ceremonies are connected with two kinds of fruit, the superior, and the inferior: in offering sacrifices, the chief fruit sought is the destruction of sin, the possession of a pure mind, and the knowledge of Bramha; the inferior fruit is, the destruction of sin, and residence with the gods for a limited period.[c] The primary object of a person in planting a tree, is the fruit; the secondary one is sitting under its shade. The chief fruit of devotion, is a fixed mind on Bramha; the inferior fruit is a temporary enjoyment of happiness with the gods. He who has obtained emancipation, does not desire this inferior fruit.

Those things which perfect the knowledge of Bramha are: 1. Discriminating wisdom, which distinguishes between what is changeable and what is unchangeable;—2. A distaste of all worldly pleasure, and of the happiness enjoyed with the gods;—3. and unruffled mind; the subjugation of the passions; unrepenting generosity; contempt of the world; the absence of whatever obstructs the knowledge of Bramha, and unwavering faith in the Véda;—4. The desire of emancipation.

Bramha, the everlasting; the everliving, is one; he is the first cause; but the world, which is his work, is finite, inanimate, and divisible. The being who is always the same, is the unchangeable Bramha, and in this form there is none else. That which sometimes exists, and at other times is not, and assumes various shapes, is finite: in this definition is included all created objects. Devotedness to God is intended to exalt the character, and to promote real happiness. If in ardent attachment to present things there be some happiness, still, through their

c. Pythagoras taught, that when it [the soul], after suffering successive purgations, is sufficiently purified, it is received among the gods."—*Enfield, page* 397.

subjection to change, it terminates in real sarrow, for as affection produces pleasure, so separation produces pain ; but devotion secures uninterrupted happiness. On this account, divine sages, who could distinguish between substance and shadow, have sought pleasure in God. Those learned men who declare that permanent happiness is to be enjoyed in the heavens of the gods, have erred, for we see, that the happiness which is bestowed in this world as the fruit of labour is inconstant; whatever is the fruit of actions, is not permanent, but changeable; therefore the wise, and those who desire emancipation, despise it.

Hearing the doctrines of the Védánta philosophy; obtaining, by inference, clear ideas of their meaning, and fixing the mind on that which is thus acquired; these three acquisitions, added to a knowledge of the rules to be observed by a student, and that power over the mind by which a person is enabled to reject every other study, is called Shama. Dama is that by which the organs and faculties are kept in subjection. If, however, amidst the constant performance of Shama and Dama, the desire after gratification should by any means arise in the mind, then that by which this desire is crushed, is called Uparati;[d] and the renunciation of the world, by a Sanyási who walks according to the Véda, is called by the same name.

Those learned men who wrote the comments on the Védánta before the time of Shankaráchárya, taught, that in seeking emancipation, it was improper to renounce religious ceremonies, but that the desire of reward ought to be forsaken; that works should be performed to obtain divine wisdom, which, being acquired, would lead to emancipation; that works were not to be rejected, but practised without being considered as a bargain, for the performance of which a person should obtain such and such benefits; that therefore works, and the undivided desire of emancipation, were to be attended to; which is illustrated in the following comparison: Two persons being on a

d Disgust.

journey, one of them loses his horse, and the other his carriage; the first is in the greatest perplexity, and the other, though he can accomplish his journey on horseback, contemplates the fatigue with dissatisfaction. After remaining for some time in great suspense, they at length agree to unite what is left to each, and thus with ease accomplish their journey. The first, is he who depends on works, and the latter, he who depends on wisdom. From hence it will be manifest, that to obtain emancipation, works and divine wisdom must be united. Formerly this was the doctrine of the Védánta, but Shankáracharya in a comment on the Bhagavat-gitá, has, by many proofs, shewn, that this is an error; that works are wholly excluded, and that knowledge alone, realizing every thing as Bramha, procures liberation.

Cold and heat, happiness and misery, honour and dishonour, profit and loss, victory and defeat, &c. are termed Dwanda. Indifference to all these changes is stiled Titikshá. This indifference, together with a subdued mind, is called Samádhi. Implicit belief in the words of a religious guide, and of the Védánta, is termed Shraddhá. This anxious wish, 'when shall I be delivered from this world, and obtain God?' is called Mumukshatwa. The person who possesses these qualities, and who, in discharging the business of life, and in practising the duties of the Véda, is not deceived, possesses the fruits of the Védânta; that is, he is adhikâri.—*Here ends the first part of the Védánta, called Adhikári.*

The next part is called Vishaya, throughout which this idea is inculcated, that the whole meaning of the Védánta are comprised in this, that Bramha and individuated spirit are one. That which, pervading all the members of the body, is the cause of life or motion, is called individuated spirit (jēēva); that which pervades the whole universe, and gives life or motion to all, is Brâmhá. Therefore, that which pervades the members of the body, and that which pervades the universe, imparting motion to all—are one. The vacuum between the separate trees in a forest, and universal space, is of the same nature; they are both pure ether; and so Bramha and individuated spirits are one; they are both pure life. That wisdom by which a person realizes that individuated spirit and Bramha are one, is called Tattwa-gnâna, or the knowledge of realities.

Bramha, the governor, or director of all things, is ever-living, unchangeable, and one; this inanimate, diversified, and changeable world, is his work. Governors are living persons; the dead cannot sustain this office; every species of matter is without life; that which is created cannot possess life. This comparison is drawn from secular concerns; and thus, according to the Véda, all life is the creator, or Bramha; the world is inanimate matter. All material bodies, and the organs, are inanimate; the appearance of life in inanimate things arises from their nearness to spirits: in this manner, the chariot moves because of the presence of the charioteer. That through the presence of which bodies and their members are put in motion, is called spirit. He is the first cause; the ever-living; the excellent God, besides whom there is none else. Therefore, in all the shastràs he is called Vishwátmá; the meaning of which is, that he is the soul of all creatures.[e] This is the meaning of the whole of the Védánta. Wherefore all [spirits] are one, not two; and the distinctions of I, thou, he, are all artificial existing only for present purposes, and through pride [Avidyà]. Though a man should perform millions of ceremonies, this Avidyà can never be destroyed but by the kowledge of spirit, that is, by Bramhagnána.[f] This Avidyá is necessary to the

e "Thales admitted the ancient doctrine concerning God, as the animating principle or soul of the world." *Enfield, page* 143. "The mind of man, according to the Stoics, is a spark of the divine fire which is the soul of the world." *Ibid page* 341.

f Krishna, in the Bhagavat-gitá, thus describes the efficacy of the principle of abstraction: "If one whose ways are ever so evil serve me alone, he is as respectable as the just man. Those even who may be of the womb of sin; women; the tribes of vaishya shudra, shall go the supreme journey, if they take sanctuary with me,"

present state only: divine knowledge secures emancipation.—That Jiva and Bramha are one is, therefore, the substance of *the second part of the Védánta.*

The third part is called Sambandha; g and teaches, that the Vèdánta contains the knowledge of Bramha and that by the Védánta the knowledge of Bràmhà may be obtained.

The fourth part, called Prayojana imports, that this part of the Védânta was written to destroy completely that illusion by which this body and this organized world were formed, and to point out the means of obtaining [re-union to] the ever-blessed Bramha. This is called liberation. A person, vexed with the necessity of transmigrations, h with anger, envy, lust, wrath, sorrow, worldly intoxication, pride &c. takes some flowers, fruits, &c. to an initiating priest, who understands the Vèdànta, and has obtained the knowledge of spirit, and requests his instructions. The guide, by endeavouring to excite in his mind a contempt of the world, leads him to the knowledge of Bramha.

Worldly attachment is thus illustrated: a person observes a string on the ground, and imagines it to be a snake: his fears are excited as much as though it were in reality a snake, and yet he is wholly under the power of error; so the hopes, fears, desires, pride, sorrow, &c. of the man who is under the influence of worldly attachment, are excited by that which has no substance; and he is therefore placed among the ignorant. But the wise, the everlasting, the blessed Bramha, is unchangeable and has no equal. All things past, present, and to come; of

---

g Union.

h The Pythagoreans taught, that "the soul of man consists of two parts; the sensitive, produced from the first principles with the elements; and the rational, a demon sprung from the divine soul of the world, and sent down into the body as a punishment for its crimes in a former state, to remain there till it is sufficiently purified to return to God. In the course of the transmigration to which human souls are liable, they may inhabit not only different human bodies, but the body of any animal or plant. All nature is subject to the immutable atd eternal law of necessity." *Enfield, page 406.*

every class and description, whether in the earth, or in the air, are Bramha, who is the cause of all things, as well as the things themselves. If it be not admitted, that he is both the potter and the clay, it will follow, that for clay (inanimate matter) he was beholden to another.

The meaning of the word Bramhâ is, the Ever Great. Molasses deposited in a quantity of rice diffuse their sweetness through the whole: so Bramha, by diffusing through them his own happiness, makes all souls happy; hence, in all the shâstràs he is called the Ever-Blessed. Wherefore the ever-blessed, the everlasting, the incomparable Bramha—he is entity. That which is without wisdom and without life, is called Awasta [non-entity].

We cannot call illusion entity, for as soon as a person obtains discriminating wisdom, illusion is destroyed; nor can it be called non-entity, for the universe which is an effect of this illusion, is an object of sight; we cannot therefore say whether it is entity or non-entity; it is something which cannot be described. This illusion resembles the temporary blindness under which the owl and other creatures labour, so that they can see nothing after the sun has arisen. This blindness cannot be called real, nor can it be unreal, for to these creatures it is real, and [during the day] constant blindness. In the same manner, illusion does not belong to the wise; but it constantly belongs to him, who, owl-like, is destitute of discriminating wisdom. This illusion is identified with Satwa, Raja, and Tama gunas: it is not merely the absence of wisdom; but as being opposed to the true knowledge of Brahma is called Adnyána. The whole mass of this illusion is one; individuated, it assumes different shapes; and in this respect resembles the trees in a forest, and single trees. The mass of illusion forms the inconceivable and unspeakable energy of God, which is the cause of all things, Individuals. God and individuated souls are life. Property and its possessor are not equivalent terms; therefore wisdom is not the energy of spirit, since wisdom and spirit are the same; but illusion forms its energy.

Light is not the ener y of spirit, since light and spirit are the same; but darkness forms its energy; not that darkness which arises from the absence of light, but that which surrounds a person in a profound sleep.

We call the mass of illusion, which equally contains the three Gunas, and in which the Satwa Guna prevails, excellent because it is the cause of all things. This mass of illusion takes refuge in the ever-living, or the ever-blessed Bramha, who is called, in the Vèdàs and all the Shástras, the all-wise, the sovereign of all, the disposer and the director of all; the accomplisher of all his desires, of all he appoints; he assumes the forms of his works; and is known as the cause of all; he knows, and, as the charioteer directs the chariot, directs the hearts of all. This mass of illusion is identified with God, and creates all things: it is the cause of vacuum and all other things which compose the atomic and material world; it is therefore called the material cause and the universal cause.

At the dissolution of the universe, all things take refuge in the aggregate of illusion; therefore the aggregate of illusion is represented by a state of deep sleep. This illusion, in its individuated state, is pervaded by the three Gunàs in equal proportions; but in individual bodies, on account of the diminutiveness of the receptacle, there is a depression of the Satwa Guna, and a greater manifestation of the other two Gunas. The living principle, which becomes that in which this individuated illusion takes refuge, is called in all the Shástras Pradánya. The state of a person in a heavy sleep, when every earthly object is excluded from the mind, is called Pradonya,or subjection to false ideas. We are not to suppose that during profound repose the soul departs; the soul is present; for when the person awakes he says, "I have been quite happy; I was not conscious of anything:" from these expressions it appears, that the person was conscious of personal existence, of happiness, and yet had no ideal intercourse with material things; for had he not previously tasted of happiness, he could have had no idea of happiness in sleep. If it be asked, from whence does this knowledge arise which a person possesses in a state of profound repose; does it not arise from the operations of the understanding? To this we answer, if this were the case, why should not the understanding be employed on outward object likewise? The fact is, that in the time of heavy sleep, the operations of the understanding are withheld, and are buried in illusion Adnyâna; but the knowledge possessed in deep sleep is constant: the Védânta identifies this knowledge with the living spirit. That during the time of profound repose pleasure is enjoyed, is proved from the care with which the bed is prepared, that comfort may be enjoyed in sleep. In the time of profound repose, all the powers are absorbed in illusion, and therefore, having no intercourse with material objects, the pleasure enjoyed at that time can have no connection with these objects. Therefore this pleasure the Vèdânta identifies with the living spirit. This then is clear, that spirit is the fulness of constant joy and knowledge. In the time of profound sleep, all material objects being thus buried in illusion, this illusion is called the co-existent energy of spirit; it is the producing cause of consciousness, of the understanding, intellect, the five senses, the five organs, the five breaths, crude matter and of all other material things; and hence the Vèdânta speaks of this energy as the material cause of all things. It is called profound repose, inasmuch as in deep sleep all things are lost in this illusion, as salt in water; or the state of our ideas in waking and sleeping hours may be compared to the projection or drawing in of the head and feet of the turtle. The absorption of all things in the mass of illusion is called the great pruluya, or destruction; and the manifestation or procession of all things from this illusion, is called creation. The illusion in which individual souls take refuge, and that in which the aggregate body of spirit, that is the Great Spirit, takes refuge, is the same, resembling individual trees and a forest. For as there is a vacuum surrounding every individual tree in a forest, and many such vacuums in the forest, and a vacuum unconnected with every thing, in which these vacuums are absorbed, so, agreeably to all the Shâstras, there is a perfect spirit in which individual souls, and the aggregate body of souls, take refuge. This perfect spirit is united to gross matter, to material things, to individual sprits, and to the aggregate of spirit, as fire to red-hot iron; and in this state it is called Eeshwa, or the glorious; when separate from these, it is called the excellent Brahma.

This illusion possesses the power of concealing an object and of deception: a small cloud darkening the sight of the person looking at the sin, appears to hide this immense luminary; so this illusion, possessing the energy of spirit, though confined within bounds, by covering the understanding, hides the boundless and unassociated living Bramha from the sight of the person who desires to know him, as though it had covered, Bramha himself. This spirit, thus covered with illusion, becomes engaged in various worlds by anxieties, as I am happy, I am miserable, I am sovereign, I am subject [to the fruits of actions]: this illusion operates in a person subject to these anxieties as it does in the case of a person deceived by a cord when he supposes it to be a snake.

This illusion, by its power of deception, after having thus covered spirit, assumes an endless variety of deceptive forms, similar to real ones, yet no more real than when a cord, a cane, the edge of a river, &c. are feared under the illusive appearance of a serpent. Exerting a similar power of illusion, it holds forth vacuum, the five primary elements, &c. &c. as spirit.

This illusion also forms the energy of spirit; and hence, when spirit as united to illusion is spoken of as chief, it is called the primary cause of all things; and when illusion is spoken of as chief, then spirit as united to illusion is called the material cause of all things thus, the spider is himself the primary and the material cause of his web: in presiding over it, he is the former, and in forming it from his own bowels, he is the latter. The ever-blessed God is, in a similar manner, by himself and by his energy, both the original and the material cause of all things; he is the potter and the clay. If we suppose another cause of things besides God, we make two causes. If it be objected, that as the potter cannot work without clay, so God could not make the world without matter, and that therefore he must have been indebted to another for his power to make the world, the Vèdânta maintains, that the one ever-blessed God is himself both the primary and the material cause of all things.

Supposing the three Gunas to exist in a state of equilibrium in the illusive energy of spirit, till, when the Tama guna is chief, and spirit is united to the power of deception in this illusion, from spirit arises vacuum; from vacuum air; from air fire; from fire water; and from water the earth.

Our ideas of the universe divide themselves into two parts, animate and inanimate; the animate is the cause of all things, the inanimate (the universe) is the work of God. Therefore all creatures possessed of life, from man downwards, are animate in consequence of the presence of the deity, as the chariot moves in consequence of the presence of the horses and the charioteer. In the bodies of all living creatures two kinds of life exist: the first, the ever-living: the second, the ever-living united to the heart. In whatever the pure spirit exists, but in which it is not united to intellect, on account of the absence of intellect, that is inanimate matter. We conjecture then from appearances, that the tama guna which prevails in gross matter must be its material cause, for the excellencies and faults of an effect must have previously existed in the material cause. The five primary elemets are from God. As in illusion the Tama-guna prevails, so in the five primary elements, of which illusion is the material cause, the guna prevails. These elements are termed subtile, archetypal, and five-fold. From the subtile elements arose subtile bodies and gross matter.

The subtile element contains seventeen parts, which united form the seminal body. These seventeen parts are, the five senses, the five organs, the understanding and thought, and the five kinds of breath. The organs of the five senses are the ears, skin, eyes, tongue, and the nose. From the satwa guna arose the ear; from the same in air, arose the skin; from the same in fire, the eye; from the same in water, the tongue, and from the same in earth, the nose. From the satwa guna in the five primary elements, arose mind, which receives four names in consequence of its different operations, which are, the understanding, thought, consciousness of self-existence, and reflection. The understanding forms decision; indecision and doubt belong to thought; that which seeks after the nature of things is called reflection; that which leads a person to think, I am learned, I am rich, I am corpulent, I am thin, I am yellow, is called consciousness of self-existence, or pride. If in this manner, however, mind be subject to four changes still reflection must be considered as being united to the understandnig, for both these faculties are employed in forming decision. Consciousness of self-existence, or pirde, belongs to thought, for both these powers are concerned in the changes which take place in the mind. Through the five senses and the mind we become acquainted with sound, touch, form, taste, and smell. The five senses and the understanding form that clothing or receptacle[i] of spirit which is made up of knowledge. Spirit thus inclosed, or in this union, says, I am sovereign, I partake [of enjoyment, &c.;] and possessed of these thoughts, it is qualified to pratice what belongs to the present and the future state. The five organs and thought form that receptacle of spirit which is wholly made up of intellect. The five organs are the mouth, the hand, the feet, the penis, and the anus; from the Rajo-guna in vacuum arose words; from that quality in air, the hands; from the same in fire, the feet; from the same in water, the anus, and from the same in earth, the penis. The five breaths are, that which is in the nostrils, that expelled downwards, that which pervades the whole body, that which ascends into the throat and is discharged at the

i The words are Vignana-maya, *fulness of knowledge*, and Kosha, *a receptacle*.

mouth, and that which promotes digestion. Some maintain, that from these five kinds of air proceed five other kinds [here follow their names; which are said to be connected with digestion, sleep, hunger, sighing, and corpulency]. The five kinds of air in the body are derived from the rajo guna in each of the five primary elements. These five kinds of air when united to the five organs form that receptacle of spirit which is entirely composed of air. This receptacle, being derived from the active principle, or Rajoguna is identified with actions. We call the first of these three receptacles, chief, because it possesses the power of giving knowledge; the second is identified with action, because it is derived from thought; the last is identified with things, because of power the action belongs to it. These three receptacles united form for the reception of spirit the subtile body. When we form an idea of all the subtile bodies, we call them the collected mass of subtile bodies, as the idea of a forest is formed when the understanding conceives of many trees at once, or when many waters suggest the idea of a lake; and separate ideas of these subtile bodies, necessarily lead us to individual substances. We compare the spirit which is united to the collected mass of subtile bodies to the thread upon which are strung the pearls of a necklace. The ever-living who is united to the knowledge-possessing mind is called creator; and as he possesses the chief power of action, he is termed breath [Pràna]. When we are awake, the object embraced by the senses and organs impress their own images on the imagination, and these images are revived in sleep; and this is the state of things with Spirit in reference to its union with these three receptacles: in the first, spirit appears as the sovereign; in the second, as the creators, and in the third, as the thing created. In the subtile body formed for Spirit out of these three receptacles, the mass of gross matter is absorbed.j When united to individual

j Gross matter is absorbed in this subtile or Linga body, and the Linga body is absorbed in illusion. Does not this doctrine resemble that of some of the Greeks, that there is no such thing as real substance, that every thing called material is merely ideal ?

subtile bodies and to the luminous imagination, we call spirit the glorious, for then he is the manifester. He [the collected mass of the Linga bodies], who is compared to the thread upon which are suspended the flowers of a garden; and who is the glorious [or he who is the individuated Linga body], in the time of sleep, enjoys the ideas which have been possessed by the mind when awake: this is also taught in the Véda. Individuated spirit differs from collective spirit only as one tree differs from a forest; or as the vacuum which surrounds each tree differs from that of a whole forest; in other words, it is a drop, or a lake. In this manner, from the five subtile elements proceeded subtile bodies. From these five subtile elements, in proportions of five, arose the masses of solid matter; but each is distinguished by the name of that element which is most prevalent. In the solid mass of either, sound is found; in air is found both sound and touch; in fire, sound, touch, and form; in water, sound, touch, form, and taste; in earth, sound, touch, form, taste, and smell. The qualities are, partly natural and partly artificial. From these five elements have sprung the seven upper worlds, the seven lower worlds the four solid bodies, food, &c. There are four kinds of bodies, viz. such as are born in the womb, and those produced from eggs, from heat, and from the earth.

The active principle dwelling in the collected sum of solid matter is called Vaishwánara, or, he who is conscious of self-existence, and Viràta, as he is held forth or displayed in all creatures. This collected sum of gross matter is called annamayakosha [the receptacle raised by food only], because it is named from its origin; and as it is the seat of action [participation] it is called Jágarana, or the active. The active principle as individuated in a sensible body is called Vishwa, which name it receives because this body enters into the three receptacles before-mentioned. We called these receptacles kosha [a sheath or scabbard] because as the silkworm is covered by its shell, so they cover spirit.

There are ten deities, regents of the senses and organs, through whom spirit enjoys the pleasures of the senses and organs: through the god of the winds, spirit enjoys the pleasures of touch, and thus through the other nine.

The animating principle pervading all bodies, from the most gross to the most ideal, is the same in all. There is no difference between the incarcerated and the perfectly abstracted spirit; the body is mere illusion.

Having thus explained the doctrine of spirit, and displayed that which is mere illusion, I shall now mention the mistakes which have arisen from the different representations which learned men have given of the incarcerated spirit. The ignorant say, that a son is spirit; and that we are taught this in the Vèda; for a father values a son as himself; when he dies, he mourns as for himself, and in the happiness of the son, enjoys happiness himself. The Charwakas maintain, as they also say, from the Véda, that this body, which owes its existence and all its changes to food, is spirit, and that a son is not spirit, since the father, when the house is on fire, abandons his son, and saves himself; and that when the father says, I am corpulent, or, I am not corpulent, he confines these expressions to himself, and never applies them to his son. Other atheists contend, from the Vèda, that the organs are spirit, since they are the medium of sound, and are possessed of motion; and that this is further proved by the exclamations, I am blind, I am deaf, &c. Other atheists endeavour to prove, from the Véda, that from bodies spirit is born, and called the animal soul; since the animal soul being gone, the organs cease to exercise their functions; it is the animal soul that says, I am thirsty, I am hungry, &c. Another pleads, that intellect is spirit, and he also quotes the Véda urging that when intellect is suspended, life itself is suspended; and that as it is by intellect and reason that men are distinguished, it is plain that intellect is spirit. The Boudhas affirm, that the understanding is spirit, since in the absence of the moving cause, the bodily powers are capable of nothing; and it is the understanding which says, I am sovereign, I am subject [to the fruit of actions]. The Prabhákaras and the Tárkikas say, quoting the Véda also that besides the understanding there is another spirit, the all-blessed; for that the understanding is absorbed in illusion. The latter add to the sentiment, that illusion is spirit. The Bhatta affirm, quoting the Véda, that the animating principle, which is united to illusion and is identified with joys, is spirit; since, in the time of deep sleep, this animáting principle is both animate and illusive-formed; for when a person says, I know not myself, he gives a proof both as consciousness and unconsciousness. Another Boudha, still acknowledging the Véda, maintains, that vacuum is spirit; because the Vèda teaches us, that before creation vacuum alone existed; that at the time of absorption nothing remains; and when a person awakes after a deep sleep [in which all material things were forgotten] he says, I was wholly unconscious of the existence of any thing.

All these sects make that spirit which is not spirit; though they pretend to argue from the Véda, from the union of spirit and matter, and from inference, yet they are supported by none of these, and they one by one confute each other. Still these atheistical writers affirm, If we err, we err with the Vèda, as well as with the two other sources of proof. The writer of the Vèdânta says, True, the Vèda contains all these opinions, but its final decision is, that spirit pervades all bodies: it is not therefore identified with a son. Spirit is not material, but ideal, and therefore is identified with body. It is unorganized, and cannot therefore be identified with the organs. It is not animal life, and therefore cannot be identified with breath. It is not intellect and therefore it cannot be identified with mind. It is not a creator [or governor] and therefore it is not to be identified with the Vidnyâna maya kosha. It is a living principle, and therefore it cannot be identified with illusion or inanimate matter. It is pure life, and therefore is not connected with inanimate matter. It is entity, and therefore must not be identified with vacuum. From hence it appears, that the opinions of these sects are at variance with the Veda, and that what they term spirit is not spirit. All inanimate things, from a son to vacuum itself, are indebted to the inanimating principle for manifestation, and from hence it appears, that they cannot be spirit; and this is still further confirmed by the Yogi the subject matter of whose meditations is, I am Bramha, simple life.

This then is the exact doctrine of Védânta, that as spirit is the principle which inanimates a son &c.; that as it is constantly perfect and free from illusion; is wisdom, that is, it must be constantly identified with knowledge; is always free or unconnected with the habits of material things; is eternal and uncreated; and is the all-pervading—it is called Atmá.

A cord, though it resembles a snake, is notwithstanding a real cord; the idea that it is a snake, is pure error. In this manner, Bramha is real entity; and the universe, which appears illusive, is indeed Bramha; in the idea that it is something different from Bramha, lies the mistake.

From the five primary elements arise all bodies, also that which nourishes all, and the fourteen worlds. From the five subtile elements, arise the five gross elements and their qualities, and the collected mass of subtile bodies. From the living principle united to illusion, arise the five subtile elements and the three gunas. From the perfect Bramha, arise illusion and the animating principle united to illusion.

The author next enters into an explanation of the tenet, that spirit in its separate state, also as united to the mass of illusion, or gross matter, and is incarcerated in separate bodies, is identically the same, and, to the Yogi, purified from illusion is really the same. Such an one thus meditates on spirit: "I am everlasting, perfect, perfect in knowledge, free from change, I am entity, the joyful, the undivided, and the one Bramha." Day and night thus meditating, the Yogi at length loses sight of the body, and destroys all illusion.

The next stage of the Yogi is that in which he renounces all assistance from the understanding, and remains without the exercise of thought; in which state every thing attached to mortal [rather intellectual] existence becomes extinct. He is now identified with Bramha, and remains as the pure glass when the shadow has left it; and thus illustrates that verse of the Vèda, that the mind is both capable and incapable of embracing Bramha.

The understanding, through the organs, in conceiving of visible objects assumes the forms of these objects, and thus destroys ignorance; after which they become manifest by the rays of spirit. Thus when a light enters a dark room, it first disperses darkness, and then discovers the objects contained in the room.

Therefore the Yogi, until he sees Bramha, ought to attend to the following duties: 1. Hearing; 2. Meditation; 3. Fixing the mind, and 4. Absorption of mind.

By the first is to be understood, hearing the doctrines of the Vèda explained, all which centre in the one Bramha. In this exercise, the student must attend to the following things; 1. Upakrama, or the beginning of the Védânta; 2. Upasanghara, or the close of the Vèdânta; 3. Abhyâsa, or committing to memory certain portions of the Vèdânta; 4. Apurvata, or, gaining from the Vèdânta perfect satisfaction respecting Bramha; 5. Phala, or the knowledge of that which is to be gained from the Védânta; 6. Art'ha-véda, or, the extolling of the fruits to be obtained from the knowledge of the Vèdanta; Upapati, or the certifying absolutely what is Brahmagnyan.—The second-thing which the student is to practise, is meditation on the one Bramha, agreeable to the rules laid down in the Vêdanta and other writings.—His third duty is, uninterrupted reflection on the invisible and only Bramha, according to the ideas contained in the Vêdanta.—The fourth effort of the student is to obtain a perfect idea of Bramha, who is wisdom in the abstract: at first, his ideas will be imperfect, and he will contemplate himself and Bramha as distinct; just as a person seeing in a horse of clay both the toy and the earth of which it is composed, cannot help retaining an idea of the thing represented by the toy. But at length his mind will become exclusively fixed on the one Bramha, the operations of the understanding being all concentrated in God, as salt when thrown into water loses its own form, and is perceptible only as water.

Those who possess this knowledge of Bramha, are in possession of or practise the eight following things, viz. 1. Yama, i. e. inoffensiveness, truth, honesty, the forsaking of all the evil in the world and the refusal of gifts except for sacrifice; 2. Niyama i. e. purity relative to the use of water after defilement; pleasure in every thing, whether prosperity or adversity; renouncing food when hungry, or keeping under the body: reading the Vèda, and what is called the worship of the mind; 3. Asana, or the posture of sitting during Yoga: 4. Pranayama, or holding, drawing in, and letting out the breath during, the repetition of incantations; 5. Pratyahara, or the power of restraining the members of the body and mind; 6. Dharana or preserving in the mind the knowledge of Bramha; 7. Dhyana, meditation; 7. Samadhi, to which there are four enemies, viz. a sleepy heart: attachment to any thing except the one Bramha; human passions, and a confused mind. When the Yogi is delivered from these four enemies, he resembles the unruffled flame of the lamp, and his mind continues invariably fixed in meditation on Bramha.

He who is distinguished by liberation in a bodily state is thus described: he possesses the knowledge which identifies him with the undivided Bramha, by which knowledge he destroys the illusion which concealed Bramha. When this illusion is destroyed, the true knowledge of Bramha is manifested; and by this manifestation, illusion and its works are destroyed, so that the free man, absorbed in meditation on Bramha, is liberated even in a bodily state. Though he is connected with the affairs of life; that is, with affairs belonging to a body containing blood, bones, ordure and urine; to organs which are blind, palsied, and full of incapacity ; to a mind, filled with thirst, hunger, sorrow, infatuation; to confirmed habits and to the fruits of birth, still, being freed from illusion, he does not view these things as realities. A person may be a spectator of the artifices of a juggler, without being deceived by them. The Yogi, after being liberated in a bodily state, still eats and drinks, but without desire; so likewise is he free from envy, and other evil desires; and in the same manner he is indifferent to every state of the body, and free from every passion. All his virtues, and the act of kindness which he performs are worn as so many ornaments, so we learn from the Gita. This Yogi, liberated in the body, for its preservation, receives aliment, but without desire, let the aliment come in whatever state, or from whatever quarter it may. Bramha alone is seen in his mind.

After this, every thing connected with a bodily state having been renounced, and the body itself having fallen, the Yogi is absorbed in the excellent Bramha; and thus illusion, and its effects, as well as the universe itself, being [to the Yogi] dissolved, he becomes identified with freedom, with constant joy, with unchangeableness, and with Bramha himself. This is recorded in the véda. *Thus ends the Vèdanta Sara.*

CREST-JEWEL OF WISDOM

OF SHRI-SANKARACHARYA

Translated by

MOHINI M. CHATTERJI F. T. S.

I prostrate myself before the true teacher—before him who is revealed by the conclusions of all systems of Vedantic philosophy, but is himself unknown, Govinda the supreme bliss.

2. Among sentient creatures birth as a man is difficult of attainment, among human beings manhood, among men to be a Brahmin, among Brahmins desire to follow the path of Vedic dharmma, and among those learning. But the spiritual knowledge which discriminates between spirit and non-spirit, the practical realisation of the merging of oneself in Brahma-atma and final emancipation from the bonds of matter are unattainable except by the good karma of hundreds of crores of incarnations.

3. These three, so difficult of attainment, are acquired only by the favor of the Gods*:—humanity, desire for emancipation, and the favor of (spiritually) great men.

4. One who, having with difficulty acquired a human incarnation and in that manhood a knowledge of the scriptures, through delusions does not labour for emancipation, is a suicide destroying himself in trying to attain illusive objects.

5. Who is there on this earth with soul more dead than he who, having obtained a human incarnation and a male body, madly strives for the attainment of selfish objects?

* Favour of the Gods is the previous karma of an individual.

6. He may study the scriptures, propitiate the gods (by sacrifices), perform religious ceremonies or offer devotion to the gods, yet he will not attain salvation even during the succession of a hundred Brahma-yugas except by the knowledge of union with the spirit.

7. The immortality attained through the acquisition of any objective condition (such as that of a god) is liable to end, as it is distinctly stated in the scriptures (Sruti) that karma is never the cause of emancipation.

8. Therefore the wise man strives for his salvation, having renounced his desire for the enjoyment of external objects, and betakes himself to a true teacher and accepts his teaching with an unshaken soul.

9. And by the practice of right discrimination attained by the path of Yoga he rescues the soul—the soul drowned in the sea of conditioned existence.

10. After giving up all karma for the purpose of removing the bonds of conditioned existence, those wise men with resolute minds should endeavour to gain a knowledge of their own atma.

11. Actions are for the purification of the heart, not for the attainment of the real substance. The substance can be attained by right discrimination, but not by any amount of karma.

12. A perception of the fact that the object seen is a rope will remove the fear and sorrow which result from the illusive idea that it is a serpent.

13. The knowledge of an object is only gained by perception, by investigation, or by instruction, but not by bathing or giving of alms, or by a hundred retentions of the breath.

14. The attainment of the object principally depends upon the qualification of him who desires to attain; all artifices and the contingencies arising from circumstances of time and space are merely accessories.

15. Therefore he who desires to know the nature of his own atma, after having reached a guru who has got Brahmagnyan and is of a kindly disposition, should proceed with his investigation.

16. One who has a strong intellect, who is a learned man and who has powers of comprehension, is a man qualified for such an investigation.

17. He only is considered worthy to enquire into spirit who is without attachment, without desire, having Sama and the other qualifications and is desirous of obtaining emancipation.

18. For this purpose there exist four kinds of preparatory training, so say the wise; with them the attempt will be successful; without them unsuccessful.

19. The first is reckoned to be the discrimination of the eternal and the transitory; then follows renunciation of the desire to enjoy the fruits of action here and hereafter.

20. Thirdly, the six possessions beginning with Sama; and fourthly, aspiration for emancipation. Brahma is true, the transitory world is a delusion; such is the form of the final conclusion which is said to be the discrimination between the transitory and the eternal.

21. Renunciation of desire consists in giving up the pleasures of sight, hearing, etc.

22. Also in giving up all pleasures derivable from all transitory objects of enjoyment from the physical body up to Brahma the creator, after repeatedly pondering over their defects and shortcomings; the undisturbed concentration of mind upon the object of perception is called Sama.

23. Dama is said to be the confinement to their own proper sphere of organs of action and of sensual perceptions, after having turned them back from objects of sense.

24. A condition not related to or depending on the external world is true Uparati.

25. The endurance of all pain and sorrow without thought of retaliation, without dejection and without lamentation, is said to be Titiksha.

26. Fixed meditation upon the teachings of Shastra and Guru with a belief in the same by means of which the object of thought is realised, is described as Sraddha.

27. Constant fixing of the mind on the pure spirit is called Samadhana. But not amusing the mind by delusive worldly objects.

28. Mumukshatva is the aspiration to be liberated by knowing one's true self from all created bonds, beginning with the feeling of personality and ending with the identification of oneself with the physical body by ignorance.

29. Even should the qualifications enumerated be possessed in a low or moderate degree, still these qualifications will be strengthened and improved by absence of desire, by Sama and the other qualities and the kinduess of the teacher, and will bear fruit.

30. In one in whom absence of desire and aspiration for emancipation are prominent, Sama and the other qualifications will be productive of great results.

31. When absence of desire and aspiration for emancipation are feeble, there will be but indications of Sama and the other qualifications, as of water in a mirage.

32. Among the instruments of emancipation the supreme is devotion. Meditation upon the true form of the real self is said to be devotion.

33. Some say devotion is meditation on the nature of one's atma. He who possesses all these qualifications is one who is fit to know the true nature of atma.

34. Such a person must approach the guru through whom freedom from bondage is attainable; one who is wise, well versed in the scriptures, sinless, free from desire, knowing the nature of Brahmham.

35. One who has attained rest in spirit, like the flame which has obtained rest when the fuel is consumed, and one whose kindness is not actuated by personal considerations, and who is anxious to befriend those that seek for help.

36. Having obtained the favour of such a preceptor through obedience and respectful demeanour, the object of one's inquiry is to be addressed to him when he is not otherwise engaged.

37. " Salutation to thee, O Lord, full of compassion, O friend of those who bend before thee. I have fallen into the ocean of birth and rebirth. Rescue me by thy never failing glance which rains the ambrosia of sincerity and mercy."

38. " Protect from death him who is heated by the roaring wild fire of changing life so difficult to extinguish, him who is oppressed and buffeted by the blasts of misfortune, since no other refuge do I know."

39. The great and peaceful ones live regenerating the world like the coming of spring, and after having themselves crossed the ocean of embodied existence, help those who try to do the same thing, without personal motives.

40. This desire is spontaneous, since the natural tendency of great souls is to remove the suffering of others just as the ambrosia-rayed (moon) of itself cools the earth heated by the harsh rays of the sun.

41. " O Lord, sprinkle me, heated as I am by the forest fire of birth and re-birth, gratify the ear with ambrosial words as they flow from the vessel of thy voice mingled with the essence of thy experience, of the pleasure afforded by Brahmagnyan, sacred and cooling. Happy are they who come into thy sight, even for a moment, for (they become) fit recipients and are accepted (as pupils).

42. " How shall I cross this ocean of birth and re-birth? What is my destiny, what means exist, O Lord, I know not. O Lord kindly protect me, lighten the sorrows arising from birth and re-birth."

43. The great soul, beholding with eyes moistened with mercy the refuge-seeker who, heated by the forest fire of birth and re-birth, calls upon him thus, instantly bids him fear not.

44. That wise one mercifully instructs in truth the pupil who comes to him desirous of emancipation, and practising the right means for its attainment, tranquil minded and possessed of Sama.

45. " Fear not, wise man, there is no danger for thee; there exists a means for crossing the ocean of birth and re-birth—that by which Yogis have crossed. I shall point it out to thee.

46. There is an effectual means for the destruction of birth and re-birth by which, crossing the ocean of changing life, thou wilt attain to supreme bliss."

47. By a proper comprehension of the purport of the Vedanta is produced the excellent knowledge; by that the great misery of birth and re-birth is terminated.

48. It is directly pointed out by the sayings of the Scriptures that Sradha, Bhakti, Dhyan and Yoga, are the causes which bring about emancipation. Whoever abides by these, attains emancipation from the bondage of incarnated existence.

49. By reason of ignorance a connection between you who are Paramatma and that which is not Atma is brought about and hence this wheel of embodied existence. By the fire of wisdom arising from this discrimination the growth of ignorance is burnt up to its very roots.

50. O Lord, in mercy hear! I am proposing a question, and when I have heard the answer from your own mouth, I shall have accomplished my end.

51. What is bondage? Whence is its origin? How is it maintained? How is it removed? What is non-spirit? What is the supreme spirit? How can one discriminate between them?

The Master said :—

52. Thou art happy, thou hast obtained thy end, by thee thy family has been sanctified, in as much as thou wished to become Brahm by getting rid of the bondage of *Avidyá*.

53. Sons and others are capable of discharging a father's debts; but no-one except one-self can remove (his own) bondage.

54. Others can remove the pain (caused by the weight of) burdens placed on the head, but the pain (that arises) from hunger and the like cannot be removed except by oneself.

55. The sick man is seen to recover by the aid of medicine and proper diet, but not by acts performed by others.

56. The nature of the one reality must be known by one's own clear spiritual perception and not through a pandit (learned man) the form of the moon must be known through one's own eye, how can it be known through (the medium of) others ?

57. Who but oneself (*atma*) is capable of removing the bondage of *Avídyá*, *Kama* and *Karma* (ignorance, passion and action) even in a thousand million of Kalpas ?*

58. Liberation cannot be achieved except by the direct perception of the identity of the individual with the universal self neither by *Yoga* (physical training), nor by *Sankhya* (speculative philosophy), nor by the practice of religious ceremonies, nor by mere learning.

59. The form and beauty of the lute (*vina*) and skin in sounding its strings are for the entertainment of the people and not for the establishment of an empire (in the hearts of subjects through the good government of the king).†

60. Good pronunciation, command of language, exegetical skill and learning, are for the delectation of the learned and not for (obtaining) liberation.

61. If the supreme truth remains unknown, the study of the scriptures is fruitless ; even if the supreme truth is known the study of the scriptures is useless (the study of the letter alone is useless, the spirit must be sought out by intuition).

62. In a labyrinth of words the mind is lost like a man in a thick forest, therefore with great efforts must be learned the truth about oneself from him who knows the truth.

63. Of what use are the Vedas to him who has been bitten by the snake of ignorance ? (Of what use are) scriptures, incantations, or any medicine except of supreme knowledge ?

---

* One day of Brahma, *i.e.*, one period of cosmic activity.

† To understand the purport of this sloka it must be remembered that the etymological derivation of the Sanscrit word for king (*Rájá*) is from the root *ráj* to please. The king was the man who pleased his subjects most. A comparison of this derivation with that of the word king from *cunan*, to know, will bring out a striking difference between the old and the Aryan Teutonic minds.

64. Disease is never cured by (pronouncing) the name of medicine without taking it; liberation is not achieved by the (pronunciation of the) word Brahm without direct perception.

65. Without dissolving the world of objects, without knowing spiritual truth, where is eternal liberation from mere external words having no result beyond their mere utterance?

66. Without the conquest of enemies, without command of the treasure of a vast country, by the mere words "I am a king," it is impossible to become one.

67. Hidden treasure does not come out at (utterance of) the simple word "out," but there must be trustworthy information, digging; and removal of stones; similarly the pure truth› itself transcending the operation of *maya* (*maya* here meaning the force of evolution) is not obtained without the instruction of the knowers of the supreme, together with reflection meditation, and so forth, and not by illogical inferences.

68. Therefore wise men should endeavour by (using) all efforts to free themselves from the bondage of conditioned existence just as (all efforts are made) for the cure of diseases.

69. The excellent question now proposed by thee should be asked by those desirous of liberation, like a sage aphorism it is in agreement with the scriptures, it is brief and full of deep import.

70. Listen attentively, O wise man, to my answer, for by listening thou shalt truly be freed from the bondage of conditioned existence.

71. The chief cause of liberation is said to be complete detachment of the mind from transitory objects; after that (the acquirement of) *sama, dama, titikshá,* and a thorough renunciation of all *karma* (religious and other acts for the attainment of any object of personal desire).

72. Then the wise student (should devote himself) daily without intermission to the study of the scriptures, to reflection and meditation on the truths therein contained ; then (finally) having got rid of ignorance the wise man enjoys the bliss of Nirvana even while on this earth.

73. The discrimination between spirit and non-spirit which it is now necessary for thee to understand, is being related by me ; listen carefully and realize it in thyself.

74, 75. The wise call this the gross body which is the combination of marrow, bone, fat, flesh, blood, chyle and semen and is made up of feet, breast, arms, back, head, limbs, and organs. It is the cause giving rise to ignorance and the delusion "I" and "my." The subtle elements are akasa, air, fire, water and earth (the higher principles of these elements are to be understood here.)

76. By mixture with one another they become the gross elements and the causes of the gross body. Their functions are the production of the five senses and these are intended for the experience of their possessor.

77. Those deluded ones who are bound to worldly objects by the bonds of strong desire, difficult to be broken, are forcibly carried along by the messenger, their own karma, to heaven *(swarga)*, earth and hell *(naraka)*.

78. Severally bound by the qualities of the five (senses) sound and the rest, five (creatures) meet with their death, viz., the deer, elephant, moth, fish and black bee ;* what then of man bound by all (the senses) jointly ?

---

* It is said that music exercises a powerful fascinating effect on the deer. We are told that ancient Indian hunters used to take advantage of this fact and attract deer by playing soft music on the flute and thus lure animals to their death. The elephant is constantly surprised and killed by hunters while in a state of stupefaction caused by the pleasure the animal derives from rubbing its forhead against the pine tree. Sanskrit writers frequently mention this circumstance. The moth and bee are respectively attracted by sight, taste and smell.

79. In point of virulence sensuous objects are more fatal than the poison of the black snake *(Naja Trupidiunus)*; poison only kills one who imbibes it, but sensuous objects can kill (spiritually) even by their mere outward appearance (literally: by the mere sight of them).

80. He who is free from the great bondage of desires, so difficult to avoid, is alone capable of liberation; not another, even though versed in the six systems of philosophy.

81. Those only sentimentally desirous of liberation and only apparently free from passion, seeking to cross the ocean of conditioned existence, are seized by the shark of desire, being caught by the neck, forcibly dragged into the middle and drowned.

82. He only who slays the shark of desire with the sword of supreme dispassion, reaches without obstacles the other side of the ocean of conditioned existence.

83. The mind becomes turbid of him who treads the rugged path of sensuous objects, death awaits him at every step like a man who goes out on the first day of the month (according to the saying of the astrologers);* but whoever treads the right path under the instruction of a guru or a good man who looks after his spiritual welfare, will obtain by his own intuition the accomplishment of his object; know this to be the truth!

84. If the desire for liberation exists in thee, sensuous objects must be left at a great distance as if they were poison, thou must constantly and fervently seek contentment as if it were ambrosia, also kindness, forgiveness, sincerity, tranquillity and self-control.

85. Whoever attends only to the feeding of his own body, doing no good to others and constantly avoids his own duty, and not seeking liberation from the bondage caused by ignorance, kills himself.

---

* There is here a play on the word *pratipada*, which means both "the first step" and "the first day.

86. He who lives only to nourish his own body, is like one who crosses a river on an alligator thinking it to be a log of wood.

87. For one desirous of liberation, desires pertaining to the body &c. lead to the great death; he who is free from such desires is alone fit to gain liberation.

88. Conquer the great death—desire for the (sake of) the body, wife, son, and so on. Having conquered it the ascetics (*munis*) enter the supreme abode of Vishnu (*i. e.* attain union with the Logos who resides in the bosom of *Parabrahm*).

89. This gross body which we condemn is made up of skin, flesh, blood, nerves, fat, marrow and bones, and is filled with filth.

90. This gross body, produced out of the five gross elements themselves produced by the quintupling process, through previous karma, is the vehicle of earthly enjoyments. In the waking state of that body gross objects are perceived.

91. The ego embodied in this through the external organs enjoys gross objects such as the various forms of chaplets of flowers, sandal-wood, woman and so forth.* Therefore it is conscious of the body in its waking state.

92. Know that this gross body, on which depend all the external manifestations of *the purusha*,† is but like the house of the householder.

93. The products of the gross (body) are birth, descrepitude, and death. Its stages of development are childhood‡ and the rest. To the body, subject to diseases, belong the innumerable

* Typical of all sensuous objects.

† This word is not to be understood here as the absolute self, but merely the embodied self. *Purusha* literally means the dweller in the city, that is in the body. It is derived from *pura* which means the city or body, and *usha* a derivative of the verb *vas* to dwell.

‡ According to the Hindus the body passes through six stages,—birth existence, growth, change, decline and death.

regulations concerning caste and condition,* as do also honour, disgrace, adulation and the like.

94. Intellect, hearing, touch, sight, smell and taste (are called) senses by reason of their conveying perceptions of gross objects. Speech, hands, feet, &c. are called organs of action because through them acts are performed.

95, 96. The *manas*, *buddhi*, *ahankriti* and *chitta*, with their functions, are called the internal instruments. *Manas* is (so called) by reason of (its) postulating and doubting; *buddhi* by reason of (its) property of (arriving at a) fixed judgment about objects; *ahankriti* arises from egotism, and *chitta*, is so-called on account of its property of concentrating the mind on one's own interest.

97. Vitality (*prána*, the second principle), by the difference of its functions and modifications becomes like gold, water † and so on, *prána*, *apâna*, *vyána*, *udána*, *samâna*.

98. The five (faculties) beginning with speech, the five (organs) beginning with the ear, the five (vital airs) beginning with *prána* the five (elements) beginning with *ákása*, *buddhi* (intellect) and the rest, *avidyâ*, (ingorance) whence *káma* (desire) and *karma* (action) constitute a body called *sukshma* (subtle) body.

99. Listen! This body produced from five subtle elements is called *sukshma* as also *linga* (characteristic) *sarira*; it is the field of desires, it experiences the consequences of *karma* (prior experience); it (with the *Karana Sarira* added) being ignorant, has no beginning, and is the *upadhi* (vehicle) of *atman*.

* There are four conditions of life: *bramacharya*, houseless celibacy; *grihasthya*, family life as a householder; *vanaprastha*, religious life in the forest; and *bhaikshya*, mendicancy. Hindu legislators have prescribed rules applicable to persons in each of these conditions.

† As gold is transformed by modifications of form into bracelets, earrings etc.; and water, by change of function, becomes steam or ice or modifies its form according to the vessel in which it is contained, so vitality receives different forms in accordance with the different functions it assumes.

100. The characteristic condition of this body is the dreamy state ; this state is distinguished from the waking state by the peculiar manner in which its senses work; in the dreamy state mind itself revives the conditions created by the desires of the waking state.

101. This body having attained the condition of the actor manifests itself. In it shines the absolute self (seventh principle) which has as its vehicle intellect (higher fifth principle) and which is unaffected by any *karma* as if an independent witness.

102. Because it (seventh principle) is free from all union, it is unaffected by the action of any *upadhi.* This *linga sarira* performs all actions as the instrument of *atma* just as the chisel and other tools (perform the actions) of the carpenter ; for this reason the *atma* is free from all union.

103. The properties of blindness, weakness and adaptability exist on account of the good or bad condition of the eye ; similarly deafness, dumbness and so on are properties of the ear and are not to be considered as belonging to the self.

104. In-breathing, out-breathing, yawning, sneezing and so forth are the actions of *prána* and the rest, say the wise men ; the property of vitality is manifested in hunger and thirst.

105. The internal organ is in communication with the path of the eye and the rest, and by reason of the specialising (of the whole) the ego* (ahankara) is manifested.

* The corporeal eye by itself is incapable of seeing, otherwise it would not cease to see at the death of the body. In reality the eye sees by reason of its connection with the self through the egotism (*ahankara*) by the concept or object which may be described as " I am the seer. " That this object is different from the egotism itself is clear from the fact that there exist other objects of a similar nature strung together or connected by the egotism such as " I am the hearer, " etc.; here it is plain that the abovementioned concepts are none of them the egotism itself, for the disappearance of the concept " I am the seer" does not involve the disappearance of the egotism which manifests through other similar concepts .

106. This ego which is the subject of enjoyment and experience is to be known as *ahankara**. It attains three conditions by association with the qualities,† satva and the rest.

107. By the agreeableness of objects it becomes happy and by the contrary unhappy; happiness and unhappiness are its properties and not of atma which is the eternal bliss.

108. Objects become dear not in themselves but by reason of their usefulness to the self because the self is the most beloved of all.

109. Therefore the atma is the eternal bliss, for it there is no pain. The bliss of the atma, dissociated from all objects which is experienced in dreamless slumber, is during waking perceived by direct cognition,‡ by instruction and by inference.

110. The supreme maya out of which all this universe is born, which is *Paramesa sakti* (the power of the supreme Lord) called *avyakta* (unmanifested) and which is the beginningless avidya (ignorance) having the three *gunas* (qualities), is to be inferred through its effects by (our) intelligence.

111. This Maya is noumenal nor phenomenal nor is it essentially both; it is neither differentiated nor is it undifferentiated nor is it essentially both; it is neither particled nor is it the unparticled nor is it essentially both; it is of the most wonderful and indescribable form.

---

* It will be seen that hitherto only sensational consciousness of objects has been treated of. But in every act of sensational consciousness is involved the consciousness of the self that experiences sensation, when I become conscious say for instance of a book there are two distinct branches into which that consciousness resolves itself. I am conscious of the book and I am conscious of the fact that I am conscious of the book. This latter branch of consciousness or reflection, consciousness or self-consciousness is egotism or ahankara.

† The qualities are *satva* or pleasure and goodness, *rajas* pain and passional, activity, *tamas* indifference or dullness. In association with these qualities, forming the three classes into which objects are divided, the egotism attains its three conditions. The excess of *satva* produces super-human conditions excess of *rajas* human and excess of *tamas* sub-human existence.

‡ Which practical psychology or occultism gives.

112. Its effects can be destroyed by the realization of the non-dual Brahman, as the illusion of the serpent in the rope is destroyed by the realization of the rope. The qualities of it are called *rajas*, *tamas* and *satva* and these are known by their effects.

113. The power of *rajas*, is extension (*vikshepa*) which is the essence of action and from which the pre-existing tendencies to action were produced, and the modifications of the mind known, as attachment and other qualities productive of sorrow are always produced by it.

114. Lust and anger, greed, arrogance, malice, aversion personality, jealousy and envy are the terrible properties of *rajas* ; therefore by this quality is produced inclination to action, for this reason *rajas* is the cause of bondage.

115. The power of *tamas* is called *avriti* (enveloping) by the force of which one thing appears as another ; it is this force which is the ultimate cause of the conditioned existence of the ego and the exciting cause for the operation of the force of extension (*Vikshepa*).

116. Even though intelligent, learned, skilful, extremely keen-sighted in self examination and properly instructed in various ways, one cannot exercise discrimination, if enveloped by *tamas*; but, on account of ignorance one considers as real that which arises out of error, and depends upon the properties of objects produced by error. Alas ! for him ! great is the enveloping power of *tamas* and irrepressible !

117. Absence of right perception, contradictory thinking, thinking of possibilities, making unsubstantial things for substance, belong to *rajas*. One associated with *rajas* is perpetually carried away by its expansive power.

118. Ignorance, laziness, dullness, sleep, delusion, folly and others are the qualities of *tamas*. One possessed by these perceives nothing correctly but remains as if asleep or like a post.

119. Pure *satva*, even though mixed with these two, in the same way as one kind of water mixes with another,* becomes the means of salvation; [for] the reflection of the absolute self (supreme spirit), received by *satva*, sunlike manifests the universe of objects.

120. The properties of mixed *satva* are self-respect, self regulation, self-control, and the rest, reverence, regard, desire for liberation, god-like attributes and abstinence from evil.

121. The properties of pure *satva* are purity, perception of the *atma* within us, supreme tranquillity, a sense of contentment, cheerfulness, concentration of mind upon the self by which a taste of eternal bliss is obtained.

122. The unmanifested (*avyaktam*) indicated by these three qualities is the (cause of) *karana sarira* (causal body) of the ego. The state of its manifestation is dreamless slumber, in which the functions of all organs and of the *Buddhi* are latent.

123. Dreamless slumber is that state in which all consciousness is at rest, and intellect (*buddhi*) remains in a latent state; it is known as a state in which there is no knowledge.

124. The body, organs, vitality, mind (*manas*), ego and the rest, all differentiations, the objects of sense, enjoyment and the rest, *ákása* and other elements composing this endless universe, including the *avyaktam* (unmanifested), are the not-spirit.

125. *Maya* all the functions of *Maya*—from *Mahat*† to the body know to be *asat* (*prakriti* or the unreal objectivity) like the mirage of the desert by reason of their being the non-ego.

126. Now I shall tell you the essential form *(swarupa)* of the supreme spirit (PARAMATMA), knowing which, man freed from bondage attains isolation (reality of being).

---

* *i.e. undistinguishably.*

† Buddhi, the first manifestation of Prakriti.

127. An eternal somewhat, upon which the conviction relating to the ego rests, exists as itself, being different from the five sheaths and the witness of the three conditions.

128. Who during waking, dreaming, and dreamless slumber knows the mind and its functions which are goodness and its absence—this is the ego.

129. Who by himself sees* everything, who is not seen by any one, who vitalizes *buddhi* and the others and who is not vitalized by them—this is the *atma*.

130. The *atma* is that by which this universe is pervaded, which nothing pervades, which causes all things to shine, but which all things cannot make to shine.

131. By reason of its proximity alone the body, the organs, *Manas* and *Buddhi* apply themselves to their proper objects as if applied [by some one else].

132. By it having the form of eternal consciousness all objects from *ahankara* to the body and pleasure and the rest are perceived as a jar [is perceived by us.]

133. This *Purusha*, the essential *atma*† is primeval perpetual, unconditioned, absolute happiness, eternally having the same form and being knowledge itself—impelled by whom speech (*vach*) and the vital airs move.

134. This unmanifested spiritual consciousness begins to manifest like the dawn in the pure heart, and shining like the midday sun in the "cave of wisdoms" (the *agnichakra* see "Places of Pilgrimage" October Theosophist) illuminating the whole universe.

135. The knower of the modifications (operations)‡ of the *manas* and *ahankriti*, of the actions performed by the body, organs and vitality present in them, as the fire is present in the iron, [heated by fire], does not act nor modify (in the same sense as the above,) nor follow (their actions).

---

* Cognises.

† Because it is manifested as itself in the manifested universe.

‡ *Viz.* Vitality, the organs, etc.

136. That eternal is not born, does not die, or grow or decay or modify, is not itself dissolved by the dissolution of this body, as space (is not dissolved) by the dissolution of the jar.

137. The supreme spirit (*paramatma*), different from *Prakriti* and its modifications, having for its essential characteristic pure consciousness shines equally in, manifests this infinity of reality and unreality, manifests* aham (the root of self) itself in the conditions, waking and the rest, as the witness (or subject) of *buddhi*.

138. O disciple, with mind under control, directly perceive this, the *atma* in thyself as—"this I am"—through the tranquility of *buddhi* cross the shoreless sea of changeful existence, whose billows are birth and death, and accomplish thy end, resting firmly in the form of Brahma.

139. Bondage is the conviction† of the "I" as being related to the non-ego; from the ignorance (or error)‡ arising out of this springs forth the cause of the birth, death, and suffering of the individual so conditioned. And it is from this (error) alone that (he) nourishes, anoints and preserves this body mistaking

---

* The original word is *vilasati*, plays. I am compelled to sacrifice in the translation, the suggestion in the original as to the absence of want and therefore of a motive for action in the absolute ego.

† The original word is *mati* which is a synonym for *buddhi*. Bondage therefore is that condition or modification of *buddhi* in which it takes the form of the error mentioned in the text. Starting from this initial modification *buddhi* secretes, larva-like, the world of objects which it reflects upon the *atma* and produces its bondage or illusive conditions. *Atma* is eternally pure and unconditioned, but through its erroneous identification with *buddhi*, secreting the illusion of objects, it becomes bound that is to say the modifications of *buddhi* become ascribable to it.

‡ The words *avidya* and *agnáná* are usually rendered "ignorance;" but it is necessary to state that in this connection the word ignorance has a meaning slightly different from the usual one. It does not mean negation of knowledge but is a positive concept as we said before. Perhaps error is a better rendering. The negative particle *a* in these words does not imply the negation of the term it qualifies but its antithesis. Thus *akarma*=evil act, *akhyati*=ill-fame &c.

the unreal for the real and gets enveloped in objects of sense in the same way as a cocoon maker *(larva)* gets enveloped in its own secretion.

140. O friend listen! The notion of ego in one deluded by *tamas* becomes strengthened in this (*asat*). From such absence of discrimination springs forth the notion* of rope in the snake. From this a mass of great suffering befalls the entertainer of such notion. Therefore the acceptance of *asat* as the "I" in bondage.†

141. The enveloping power of *tamas* completely enshrouds this *atma*, having infinite powers (*Vibhava*), manifested by the indivisible, eternal, non-dual power of knowledge, as *Rahu* (the shadow of the moon) enshrouds the sun's orb.

142. On the disappearance of the supremely stainless vadiance of one's atma, the deluded individual imagines the body which is not self to be self. Then the great power of *rajas* called *vikshepa* (extension) gives great pain to this individual by the ropes of bondage [such as] lust, anger, etc.

143. This man of perverted intellect, being deprived of the real knowledge of the *atna* through being devoured by the shark of great delusion, is subject to conditioned existence on account of this expansive energy (*vikshepa*). Hence he, contemptible in conduct, rises and falls in this ocean of conditioned existence, full of poison.

144. As clouds produced (*i.e.*, rendered visible) by the rays of the sun manifest themselves by hiding the sun, so egotism

---

* The original word is *dhishana*. It signifies that sub-conscious octivit which goes on during the vivid cognition of any particular state of consciousness and becomes realized in the succeeding state. Thus the *dhishana* of waking consciousness becomes real and objective in dream-life. See Sankara's Commentary on the opening Stanza of Gaurapada's *karika* on the Mandukya Upanishad.

† In other words bondage is the condition in which the notion of *I* has any content which is objective, in the largest sense of the word. But as there are grades of liberation this definition of bondage is to be taken as the absolute limit.

arising through connection with the *atma* (or ego) manifests itself by hiding the real character of the *atma* (or ego).

145. As on the unpropitious day when thick clouds devour the sun, sharp cold blasts torment the clouds, so when the ego is without intermission enveloped by *tamas* the man with deluded *buddhi* is, by the intense expansive power [*vikshepa*,] goaded on with many sufferings.

146. By these two powers is produced the bondage of the individual; deluded by these two he thinks the body to be the *atma*.

147. Of the tree of conditioned life truly the seed is *tamas*, the sprout is the conviction that the body is the ego, attachment is the leaf, karma truly is the sap, the body is the trunk, the vital airs are the branches of which the tops are the organs, the flowers the objects [of the organs], the fruit the variety of sufferings from manifold *karma*, and *jiva** is the bird that feeds.

148. The bondage of non-ego, rooted in ignorance, produces the torrent of all birth, death, sickness, old-age and other evils of this (the *jiva*), which is in its own nature manifest without beginning or end.

149. This bondage is incapable of being severed by weapons of offence or defence, by wind, or by fire or by tens of millions of acts,† but only by the great sword of discriminative knowledge, sharp and shining, through the favour of *Yoga*.‡

150. For a man having his mind fixed upon the conclusions of the Vedas (there is) the application to the duties prescribed for him; from such application comes the self-purification of the *jiva*. In the purified *buddhi* is the knowledge of the supreme ego and from that is the extinction of conditioded life down to its roots.

---

* *Individual ego.*

† Religious socrifices, etc.

‡ *Dhatuh* is used in this sense in several Upanishads also.

151. As the water in the tank covered by a collection of moss does not show itself, so the *átma* enveloped by the five sheaths, produced by its own power and beginning with the *annamaya*, does not manifest itself.

152. Upon the removal of the moss is seen the pure water capable of allaying heat and thirst, and of immediately yielding great enjoyment to man.

153. When the five sheaths are removed the pure *pratyag-atma* (the Logos), the eternal happiness, all-pervading, the supreme light itself shines forth.

154. A wise man must acquire the discrimination of spirit and not spirit; as only by realising the self which is absolute being, consciousness and bliss, he himself becomes bliss.

155. Whoever, having discriminated the *pratyagatma* that is without attachment or action, from the category of objects, as the reed is discriminated from the tiger-grass, and having merged everything in that, finds rest by knowing that to be the true self, he *is emancipated** by recognition of the *pra-tyagatma* and transfer of the human individuality to it.

156, 157. This food-produced body, which lives through food and perishes without it, and is a mass of skin, epidermis, flesh, blood, bone, and filth, is the *annamaya* sheath: it cannot be regarded as the self which is eternal and pure.

158. This (átma) was before birth and death and is now: how can it, the true self, the knower of condition† and modification, be ephemeral, changeable, differentiated, a mere vehicle of consciousness?

159. The body is possessed of hands, feet, and the rest; not so the true self which, though without limbs, by reason of its being the vivifying principle and the indestructibility of its various powers, is the controller and not the controlled.

---

* *i.e.* By recognition of the *pratyagátma* (logos) as the individuality in man.

† The original word *bhava* would perhaps be better explained as the stable basis ot modifications.

160. The true self being the witness of the body and its properties, its actions and its conditions, it is self evident that none of these can be a characteristic mark of the atma.

161. Full of misery, covered with flesh, full of filth, full of sin, how can it be the knower? The ego is different from this.

162. The deluded man considers the ego to be the mass of skin, flesh, fat, bones and filth. The man of discrimination knows the essential form of self, which is the supreme truth, to be without these as characteristic marks.

163. "I am the body"—such is the opinion of a deluded man; of the learned the notion of *I* is in relation to the body, as well as to the *jiva* (monad). Of the great soul possessed of discrimination and direct perception, "I am Brahman," such is the conviction with regard to the eternal self.

164. O you of deluded judgment, abandon the opinion that the ego consists in the mass of skin, flesh, fat, bone, and filth; know that the real self is the all-pervading, changeless àtma, and so obtain peace.

165. As long as the wise man does not abandon the notion that the ego consists of the body, organs and the rest, the product of illusion, so long there is no prospect of his salvation, even though he be acquainted with the Vedas and their metaphysical meaning.

166. As one's idea of *I* is never based on the shadow or reflection of the body, or the body seen in dream or imagined by the mind, thus also may it be with the living body.

167. Because the false conviction that the ego is merely the body is the seed producing pain in the form of birth and the rest, pains must be taken to abandon that idea; the attraction towards material existence will then cease to exist.

168. Conditioned by the five organs of action, this vitality becomes the *pranamaya* sheath through which the embodied ego performs all the actions of the material body.

169. The *pránamaya*, being the modification of life-breath and the comer and goer, in and out, like air-currents, is also not the *átma*, because it cannot by itself discriminate between good and evil, or the real self and another, it is always dependent on another (the self).

170. The organs of sensation together with the *manas* form the *manomaya* sheath which is the cause (hetu) of the differentiation between I and mine; it is the result of ignorance, it fills the former sheath and it manifests its great power by distinguishing objects by names, etc.

171. The fire of the *manomaya* sheath, fed with objects as if with streams of melted butter by the five senses like five Hotris*, and blazing with the fuel of manifold desires, burns this body, made of five elements.

172. There is *avidyá* besides the *manas*. *Manas* itself is the *avidyá*, the instrument for the production of the bondage of conditioned existence. When that *(avidya)* is destroyed, all is destroyed, and when that is manifested, all is manifested.†

173. In dream, when there is no substantial reality, one enters a world of enjoyment by the power of the *manas*. So it is in waking life, without any difference, all this is the manifestation of the *manas*.‡

174. All know that when the *manas* is merged in the state of dreamless slumber nothing remains. Hence the contents of

---

* Priests offering oblations to the fire.

† *Manas* being the organ of doubt or the production of multiplicity of concepts in relation to one and the same objective reality, is here taken to be the same as *avidyá*. The *buddhi* determines these *manas* born concepts as real and through the *ahankara* specialises them by an association with the true ego. Thus is the world of illusions produced. It will now be seen that if the *manas* attains tranquillity, the world of illusions is destroyed. For then the *buddhi* having no hypothetical concepts with regard to the one objective reality to deal with, reflects that reality and the *ahankara* is destroyed by the destruction of its limitations, and becomes merged in the absolute self.

‡ See Mr. Keightley's Synopsis of Du Prel's "Philosophie der Mystik."—*Theosophist*, Vol. VI—for the psychology of dreams.

our consciousness are created by the *manas* and have no real existence.

175. Cloud collects by the wind* and is again dispersed by the wind; bondage is created by the *manas*, and emancipation is also produced by it.

176. Having produced attachment to the body and all other objects, it thus binds the individual as an animal is bound by a rope, afterwards having produced aversion to these as if to poison, that *manas* itself frees him from bondage.

177. Therefore the *manas* is the cause of the bondage of this individual and also of its liberation. The manas when stained by passion is the cause of bondage, and of liberation when pure devoid of passion and ignorance.

178. When discrimination and dispassion predominate, the *manas* having attained purity becomes fit for liberation, therefore these two (attributes) of a man desirous of liberation and possessed of *buddhi*, must at the outset be strengthened.

179. In the forest land of objects wanders the great tiger named *manas*, pure men desirous of liberation, do not go there.

180. The *manas*, through the gross body and the subtle body of the enjoyer, creates objects of desire and perpetually produces differences of body, case, condition, and race all results of the action of the qualities.

181. The *manas* having clouded over the absolute consciousness which is without attachment, it acquires notions of "I" and "mine," and through attachment to the body, organs, and life, wanders ceaselessly in the enjoyment of the fruit of his actions.

182. By ascribing the qualities of the *atmá* to that which is not *atmà* is created (the series of incarnations). This as-

---

* The word translated wind includes the atmosphere, together with its moisture and currents.

cription is produced by the *manas*, which is the primary cause of birth, suffering etc. in a man devoid of discrimination and tainted by *rajas* and *tamas*.

183. Therefore learned men who have seen the truth call the *manas avidya*, by which the universe is made to wander as the clouds are by the wind.

184. For this reason pains should bo taken to purify the *manas* by one desirous of liberation. It being purified, liberation is at hand.

185. Through the sole desire of liberation having rooted out attachment to objects and renounced personal interest in action; with reverential purity, he who is devoted to study (*sravana*) and the rest, shakes off mental passion.

186. Even the *manomaya* (sheath) is not the supreme ego on account of its having beginning and end, its modificable nature, its pain-giving characteristics, and by reason of its being objective. It is not seen by that which is itself seen (or objective) for it is the seer (or subject),

187. The *buddhi* with its functions and combined with the organs of perception becomes the *vignanamaya* sheath whose characteristic is action and which is the cause of the revolution of births and deaths.

188. The modification of prakriti (to-gether with) the power accompanying *chita pratibimba* (jiva or monad) is called *vignanamaya* the atma, and is possessed of the faculties of cognition and action,* and its function is to specialise the body, *organs* and the rest as the ego.

189. This (ego) having no beginning in time is the jiva or monad. It is the guide of all actions, and governed by previous desires, produces actions, righteous and unrighteous and their consequences.

---

* For explanation of *gnanasakti* (faculty of cognition) and *kriyasakti* (faculty of action) see Five years of Theosophy, pp. 110—1.

190. It gathers experience by wandering through various grades of incarnation* and comes below and goes above† It is to this *vignânamaya* that belongs the pleasure and pain, pertaining to waking, dreaming and the other conditions.

191. Pre-eminently illumined by the light (of the Logos) on account of its close proximity to the *Parátma* (the Logos) the *vignânamaya* sheath which produces the difference between "I" and "mine" and all actions pertaining to different stages of life and condition becomes its *upadhi* (objective basis) when *jiva* passes from one existence to another through ignorance.

192. This clothed in the *vignànamaya* sheath shines in the vital breaths (subtle currents of the *sukshmasarira)* and in the heart.‡ This atma acting on *Kuthastha* (*mulaprakriti*) and manifesting in this *upadhi* appears to be the actor and enjoyer.

193. Being limited by (*buddhi*) (intellect) the atma though pervading all appears different (from other objects) through the illusive nature (the ego), just as the water-jar and the rest (appear different) from the earth.

194. *Parátmá* by reason of connection with an objective basis, appears to partake of the attributes (of this *upadhi*) just as the formless fire seems to partake of the form of the iron (in which it inheres). The *atma* is, by its very nature, essentially unchangeable. The pupil said.

195. Whether through ignorance or any other cause, the *atma* invariably appears as *jiva* (higher portion of fifth principle); this *upadhi*, having no beginning, its end cannot be imagined.

---

* Such as animal, human, etc.

† Objective and subjective conditions.

‡ The seat of abstract thought.

196. Hence the connection of the *atma* with *jiva* does not seem to be terminable, and its conditioned life appears to be eternal, then tell me, O blessed Master, how there can be liberation? The blessed teacher said :—

197. O wise man: you have asked rightly. Now, listen carefully. The illusive fancies arising from error are not conclusive.

198. Without error truly the *atma*, the independent and non-acting, and formless cannnot be connected with objects, just as blue colour is attributed to the sky (on account of our limited vision.)

199. The seer of the self (*pratyagatma*), being without action, without attributes, is knowledge and bliss. Through the error (caused by) *buddhi* it appears conditioned (connected with *jiva*) but this is not so. When this error is dispelled, it no longer exists, hence it is unreal by nature.

200. As long as there is this error, so long this (connection with *jiva*) created by false knowledge, exists; just as the illusion, produced by error, that the rope is the snake, lasts only during the period of error—on the destruction of error no snake remains—it is even so.

201, 202. Ignorance has no beginning, and this also applies to its effects; but upon the production of knowledge, ignorance although without beginning, is entirely destroyed as is everything of dream life upon awakening. Even though without beginning this is not eternal, being clearly analogous to *pragabhava*.*

203, 204. The connection of the *atma* with *jiva*, created through its basis, *buddhi*, though having no beginning, is thus seen to have an end. Hence this connection does not exist,

---

* Antecedent non-existence. Cf. Nyaya philosophy for explanation of this term e.g. the state of a pot before manufacture is one of antecedent non-existence.

and the *atma* is entirely different from the *jiva* in nature and attributes. The connection between *atma* and *buddhi* (mind) is established through false knowledge.

205. This connection can only be terminated by true knowledge—it cannot be otherwise. The knowledge that *Brahm* (the first cause) and *atma* are one and the same is true knowledge and according to the Vedas.

206. This knowledge can only be acquired by the perfect discrimination of ego and non-ego; after that discrimination is to be practised in relation to *pratyagatma* (the Logos) and *sadatma* (the ego).

207, 208. As the most muddy water appears pure water on the removal of the mud, even so the *pratyagatma* shines clearly when *sadátma* (the ego) is removed from unreality asat.* Therefore the Logos should be separated from *sadátma* and all that pertains to the false self.

209. Hence the *Paratma* (the Logos) is not that which is called the *vignanamaya*. By reason of its changeable, detached character and materiality, as well as on account of its objectivity and liability to error, it (*Vignanamaya sheath*) cannot be regarded as eternal.

210. *Anandamaya sheath* is the reflection of the absolute bliss, yet not free from ignorance. Its attributes are pleasure and the like, through it the higher affections are realised (e. g. in *swarga*). This *sheath*, whose existence depends upon virtuous action, becomes manifest as *Anandamaya* without effort (that is, as the necessary result of a good life) in a virtuous man enjoying the fruits of his own merit.

211. The principal manifestation of the *Anandamaya* sheath is in dreamless slumber. In the waking and dreaming states it becomes partially manifested at the sight of pleasant objects.

212. Nor is this *Anandamaya* Paratma (the Logos) the supreme spirit, because it is subject to conditions. It is a modification of *Prakriti*, an effect, and the sum of all the consequences of good acts.

*This refers to the upadhis.

213. By inference and according to the Vedas the *atma* is what remains after the subtraction of the five sheaths. It is the witness, it is absolute knowledge.

214. This *atma* is self-illumined and different from the five sheaths; it is the witness of the three states (waking, dreaming and dreamless sleep); it is stainless, and unchanging, it is eternal bliss and thus it must be realised by the learned Brahman. The pupil said:—

215. When the five sheaths are subtracted on account of their unreality, I do not see, O Master, that any thing remains but universal negation. What, then, remains to be known by the learned Brahman, as ego and non-ego? The Master said:—

216. O wise man, thou hast spoken well, thou art skilful in discrimination, *atma* is that which is void of all changeful things, such as egotism, etc.

217. That by which everything is known, that which is not known by anything—through the subtle intellect, realize that knower to be the atma.

218. Whoever knows anything is the witness thereof. With regard to an object not perceived by any one, the characteristic of being—the witness—can be rightly postulated of none.

219. The fact that oneself is the witness is perceived by oneself. Therefore *Pratyagatma* (the Logos) is itself the witness and not another.

220. The manifestation of this *Pratyagatma* is identical in the states of waking, dreaming and dreamless slumber; it is the one inward manifestation of self-consciousness in all egos; and is the witness of all forms and changes, such as egotism, intellect, etc., and manifests itself as *chidatma* (real self) and eternal bliss. This realize as *Pratyagatma* in your own heart.

221. The fool, having seen the image of the sun in the water of the jar, thinks it is the sun. So an ignorant man

seeing the reflection of the logos in any of the *upadhis* (vehicles), takes it to be the real self.

222. As the wise man looks at the sun itself and not the jar, the water, or the reflection; so also the wise man looks towards the self-illumined *Pratyagatma* which shines in the three upadhis but does not partake of their functions.

223, 224. Thus it is that the individual, abandoning the body, the intellect and the reflection of *jiva* (ego) becomes sinless, passionless and deathless by knowing the all-illuminating *atma,* which is the seer, which is itself the eternal knowledge, different from reality as well as unreality, eternal, all pervading, supremely subtle, devoid of within and without, the only one, in the centre of wisdom.

225. The wise man (who becomes *Pratyagatma* by knowing it), is free from grief and filled with bliss. He fears nothing from anywhere. Without knowledge of the true self there is no other path open to those desirous of liberation for removing the bondage of conditioned life.

226. The realization of the oneness of *Brahm* is the cause of liberation from conditioned existence; through which the only *Brahm,* which is bliss, is obtained by the wise.

227. The wise man, becoming *Brahm,* does not return to conditioned existence; hence the unity of the self with *Brahm* must be thoroughly realized.

228. *Brahm* which is truth, knowledge and eternity, the supreme, pure, self-existing, uniform, eternal bliss, always pre-eminent.

229. By the absence of all existence besides itself this *Brahm* is truth, is supreme, the only one; when the supreme truth is fully realized nothing remains but this.

230. By reason of ignorance this universe appears multiform, but in reality all this is *Brahm,* (which remains) when all defective mental states have been rejected.

231. The water-pot which is the effect* of clay is yet not different from the clay, its essential nature always remaining clay. The form of the water-pot has no independent existence but is only a name generated by illusion.†

232. By no one can the water-pot be seen as itself and distinct from the clay. Therefore the water-pot is imagined from delusion; the clay alone is essentially real.

233. All products of *Brahm*, which is reality, are themselves also real; and there is nothing different from it. Whoever says that there is (anything different,) is not free from illusion but is like a man talking in his sleep.

234. *Brahm is* this universe—such is the saying of the excellent *sruti* of the Atharva Veda. Therefore all this universe is but *Brahm*, what is predicated of it as separate from *Brahm* has no existence.

235. If this universe is a reality, then the *atma* is finite, the Vêdas have no authority and want of veracity is attributed to *Ishwara* (the logos). These three things cannot be accepted by great souls.

236. The Lord, the knower of all objects in their reality, has declared, "I am not supported by these phenomenal manifestations, nor are they within me."

237. If this universe is a reality, it should be perceived in dreamless slumber. Since, however, nothing is perceived (in that condition) it is as unreal as dreams.

238. Therefore there is no real existence of the universe distinct from the *Paratma*; its distinct perception is as unreal as that of the serpent in the rope. What reality can there be in that which is merely manifest through ignorance?

239. Whatever is perceived through error by an ignorant person is nothing but *Brahm*—the silver is truly but the

---

* Effect = product.

† An empty abstraction with no substance to correspond to it.

mother-of-pearl.* In this way *Brahm* is ever and again invested with forms, but they are nothing but mere names ascribed to *Brahm*.

240. Therefore the supreme *Brahm* is the one reality, without a second, it is pure wisdom, the stainless one, absolute peace without beginning and without end, void of action and the essence of ceaseless bliss.

241. When all the differences created by *maya* (illusion) have been rejected, (there remains) a self-illumined something which is eternal, fixed, without stain, immeasurable, without form, unmanifested, without name, indestructible.

242. The wise know that as the supreme truth which is absolute consciousness, in which are united the knower, the known and the knowledge, infinite and unchangeable.

243. *Ahammahas* (the true self or the Logos clothed in its own light) is (a manifestation of) all-pervading Parabrahm which can be neither taken hold of nor abandoned, inconceivable by the mind and inexpressible by speech immeasurable, without beginning, without end.

244. *Brahm* and *atma* which are respectively designated by the terms 'that' and 'thou,' are fully proved to be identical when investigated by the light of Vedic teaching such as *tatwamasi*.†

245. The identity of the two thus indicated and predicated, cannot be proved on account of mutually exclusive attributes (that is, when the light of the Logos is manifested in *upadhis* as the *jiva* or ego) any more than that of the fire-fly and the sun, of the king and the slave, of the well and the ocean, of the atom and the mountain *(Meru)*.

---

* In reference to the well-known analogy of the erroneous perception of the mother-of-pearl as silver.

† This great aphorism of the Upanishads is formed of three words *tat* (that, *Parabrahm*) *twam* (thou, *jiva* or ego) as (art the) Logos or Ishwara.

246. The distinction is created by conditions *(upadhis)*, which in themselves are unreal. Listen this *Maya* (*Mulaprakriti*) of the logos *(Ishwara)* is the cause of *Mahat* (the first differentiation of *Mulaprakriti*) and the five sheaths are the effect of *jiva* (ego).

247. When these two *upadhis*—those of the *Para* (the Logos) and the *jiva*—are completely rejected, there is neither Para nor *jiva*. The king has his kingdom, the warrior his arms; on the removal of these there is neither king nor warrior.

248. Hence the *sruti* (Vedas) says that the quality created (by illusion) in *Brahm* is eliminated through knowledge, then *atma* and *jiva* disappear.

249. Through logical inferences having rejected as unreal every conception of what is visible, created by mind like the notion of the serpent (imagined) in the rope, or like (things seen in) dream; the identity of *atma* with *Brahm* is realized.

250. Therefore, having ascertained these attributes, their identity is established just as that of a figure of speech which loses its original meaning and takes an additional sense. But in order to realize this identity, neither the literal nor the figurative signification is to be lost sight of, both must be united in order to realize the identity of the logos and *parabrahm*. (Harmony must be sought in the analogy of contraries).

251. 'That Devadatta is myself,'—here the identity is indicated by the rejection of the contrary attributes of the terms. Similarly in the saying, 'that thou art,' rejecting the contrary attributes in both terms, identity is established.

252. The wise know the perfect identity of the *atma* with *parabrahm*. In hundreds of great aphorisms is declared the identity of *Brahm* and the *atma*.

253, 254. Renounce the false conception you have formed and understand through thy purified intellect that thou (*atma*) art *that* subtle, self-existent, *Brahm* which is perfect knowledge and indefinable as ether.

255. Just as the pot made from clay is to be considered clay, so *Sadatma* (the ego) evolved out of *Sat* (Parabrahm), is to be regarded as *sat*, and every thing is *sat*, and there is nothing existing apart from it; therefore thou art 'that'—absolute peace, without stain, great,—*Brahm* without a second.

256. Just as in dreams the place, time, objects and intellection are all unreal, so also this world, created by ignorance is unreal, and so are also this body, senses, vital airs, egoism, etc. Therefore understand thou art 'that'—absolute peace, without stain, great,—*Brahm* without a second.

257. Realize that thou art 'that'—*Brahm* which is far beyond caste, wordly wisdom, family and clan, devoid of name form, qualities and defects, beyond time, space and objects of consciousness.

258. Realize that thou art 'that'—*Brahm* which is supreme, beyond the range of all speech, but which may be known through the eye of pure wisdom. It is pure, absolute consciousness, the eternal substance.

259. Realize that thou art 'that'—*Brahm* which is untouched by the six human infirmities*; it is realised in the heart of Yogis,† it cannot be perceived by the senses, it is imperceptible by intellect or mind.

260. Realize that thou art 'that'—*Brahm* on which rests the world, created through ignorance, it (*Brahm*) is self-sustained, it is different from (relative) truth, and from untruth, indivisible, beyond mental representation.

261. Realize that thou art 'that'—*Brahm* which is devoid of birth, growth, change, loss of substance, disease and death, indestructible, the cause of the evolution of the universe, its preservation and destruction.

262. Realize that thou art 'that'—*Brahm* which is the cessation of all differentiation, which never changes its nature and is as unmoved as a waveless ocean, eternally unconditioned and undivided.

---

* Hunger, thirst, greed, delusion, decay and death.

† *i.e.*, in *Samadhi*.

263. Realize that thou art 'that'—*Brahm* which is the one only reality, the cause of Multiplicity, the cause that eliminates other causes, different from the law of cause and effect.

264. Realize that thou art 'that'—*Brahm* which is without modification, very great, indestructible, the supreme, different from all destructible elements and the indestructible logos, eternal, indestrucible bliss, and free from stain.

265. Realize that thou art 'that'—*Brahm*, that reality which manifests as many through the illusions of name, form, qualities, change, but is yet ever unchanged like gold (in the various forms of golden ornaments.)

266. Realize that thou art 'that'—*Brahm* which alone shines, which is, which is the one essence and beyond the logos, all-pervading, uniform, truth, consciousness, bliss, having no end, indestructible.

267. By known logical inferences and by intuition realize thyself as *Brahm*, just as the meaning of a sentence is understood; the certainty of this truth will be established without doubt just as (the certainty of) the water in the palm of the hand.

268. Having realized the supremely pure truth, which is perfect knowledge, remaining ever constant in the *atma* as a king in battle depends on his army, merge this objective universe in *Brahm*.

269. *Brahm*, the truth, the supreme, the only one, and different from both (relative) truth and untruth, is in the centre* of wisdom; whoever dwells in that centre has no rebirth.

270. Even if the substance (or truth) is intellectually grasped, the desire which has no beginning (expressed in the words) "I am the actor and also the enjoyer" is strong and firm, and is the cause of conditioned existence. That desire may be got rid of with great effort by the knowledge of the

---

*Literally the cavity between the eye-brows.

Logos. The sages on earth call the getting rid of that desire (literally thinning away, desire being compared to a rope) emancipation.

271. The erroneous conception that attributes one thing to another, such as that *atma* is the agoism, body, senses, etc. must be rejected by the wise through devotion to *atma*.*

272. Knowing that *atma* as the witness of mind and its operation, and having realized through pure conduct, that *atma* is the self; abandon the perception of non-spirit as spirit.

273. Having given up following the way of the world, the body, or the scriptures, remove the erroneous conception that *atma* is *non-atma*.

274. Owing to a person's desire for the things of the world, the scriptures and the body, true knowledge cannot be produced.

275. This cruel trinity of desire is called by those who know the iron chain that binds the feet of one aspiring for liberation from the prison-house of conditioned existence; he who is free from this attains liberation.

276. As by mixture with water and by friction, sandal-wood emits an excellent odour, removing all bad smells; so divine aspiration becomes manifest when external desire is washed away.

277. Aspiration towards the supreme *atma* is covered by the dust of fatal desires lurking within, but becomes pure and emits a fine odour by the friction of wisdom just as the sandal-wood (emits odour.)

278. The aspiration towards *atma* is stifled by the net of unspiritual desires, for by constant devotion to *atma* they are destroyed, and divine aspiration becomes manifest.

279. In proportion as the mind becomes firm by devotion to *atma*, it renounces all desires for external things; when all desires are completely exhausted, the realization of *atma* is unobstructed.

---

*Cp. Light on the path.

280. By constant rest in the *atma* the (individualized) mind of the Yogis disappears and desires are exhausted; therefore remove the erroneous conception that not-spirit is spirit.

281. The quality of *tâmas* is eliminated by the other two qualities,—*rajas* and *satwa*,—*rajas* by *satwa* and *satwa* by purified *satwa*; therefore, having recourse to *satwa*, remove the erroneous conception that not-spirit is spirit.

282. Having ascertained that the body cherishes past *karma*, become firm and calm and with great efforts remove the erroneous conception that not-spirit is spirit.

283. By realizing "I am not *jiva* but *Parabrahm*," remove the erroneous conception that not-spirit is spirit, which is produced by the force of desire.

284. Having understood from the scripture, from logical reasoning and from experience, the all-pervading nature of *atma*; remove the erroneous conception that not-spirit is spirit which is produced through fallacious reasoning.

285. For the *muni* (ascetic) there is no activity concerning giving or taking, therefore by devotion to the one, diligently remove the erroneous conception that not-spirit is spirit.

286. In order to strengthen the conviction of self-identity with *Brahm*, remove the erroneous conception that not-spirit is spirit through the knowledge of the identity of self and *Brahm* which arises from such sentences as 'thou art that.'

287. So long as the notion 'I am this body' is not completely abandoned, control yourself with great concentration, and with great effort remove the erroneous conception that not-spirit is spirit.

288. O wise man! so long as the notion remains that there is *jiva* and the world, even but as a dream; without interruption remove the conception that not-spirit is spirit.

289. Without allowing any interval of forgetfulness through sleep, news of worldly affairs, or the objects of sense, meditate on the self in the self.

290. Having quitted this body which is composed of flesh and impurities and produced from the impurities of father and mother, as (one quits) an outcaste; become *Brahm* and attain *the* end.

291. Having merged the ego in the Logos even as the space occupied by the water-jar is merged in free space; remain for ever silent in that state O ascetic.

292. Having become the self-illumined *Paramatma* (the Logos) on which every thing rests through *sadatma* (ego) the macrocosm is to be abandoned as well as the microcosm, like a pot containing foul matter.

293. Having transferred the concept of individuality or ego as inhering in the body, to *chidatma* (real self) which is truth and bliss and having abandoned the *lingasariram* (astral body) become for ever one (with the Logos).

294. Realizing as the " I" (the Logos) am (a manifestation of) *Brahm* in which this universe is reflected as a city in the mirror, thou shalt attain the final object.

295. Having attained that primeval consciousness, absolute bliss, of which the nature is truth, which is without form and action, abandon this illusive body that has been assumed by the *atma* just as an actor (abandons) the dress (put on.)

296. The objective universe is false from (the stand point of) the logos, and this (objective universe) is not "I" (logos) because only transitory. How then can the concept "I know all" be established with regard to transitory objects (such as) egoism and the rest?

297. *Aham Padartha* (the logos) is the witness of the egoism and the rest as its being is always perceived—even in dreamless sleep; and the scripture itself calls (it) unborn and eternal; therefore the *Pratyagatma* is different from (relative) truth and untruth.

298. The eternal unchangeable logos alone can be the knower of all differentiations of those which are differentiated.

The character of these two (differentiable and differentiation) is unreal because repeatedly and clearly perceived in the desires of mind (waking state) in dream and in dreamless sleep.

299. Therefore abandon the notion of "I" in connection with a mass of flesh as also this notion itself which is a product of *Buddhi.* But having known the *atma* which is perfect knowledge, which is affected by neither past, present nor future attain peace.

300. Abandon the notion of "I" in family, clan, name, form and state of life, which all depend on this physical body and also having abandoned the properties of the *linga sarira* such as the feeling of being the actor and the rest—become the essential form which is absolute bliss.

301. There are other obstacles which are perceived to be the cause of a man's embodied existence. Of these the first is the modification called *ahankára* (egoism).

302. So long as one is connected with the vile *ahankára* (egoism), there is not the least indication of *mukti* (final emancipation) which is a strange (thing to him).

303. He who becomes free from the shark of *ahankara* attains the essential form which is self-illumined, stainless as the moon, all-pervading, eternal bliss.

304. He who through bewildering ignorance is deprived of the firm conviction that I (the real self) am He (the Logos) realizes the identity of *Brahm* with *Atma* on the complete destruction (of ignorance).

305. The ocean of supreme bliss is guarded by the very powerful and terrible snake *ahankára,* which envelopes the self with its three heads, the *gunas.* The wise man is able to enjoy the ocean of bliss after cutting off, these three heads and destroying this serpent with the great sword of spiritual knowledge.

306. So long as there is the least indication of the effects of poison in the body, there cannot be freedom from disease. In like manner the ascetic (Yogi) will not gain *mukti* so long as there is egoism.

307. By the complete cessation of egoism and the (consequent) extinction of all its deceitful manifestations, this essential truth—'This I am'—is realized through discrimination of the real self.

308. Abandon at once the notion of *I* in the *ahankára* which is the cause of change, which experiences the consequences of Karma, and which is the destroyer of rest in one's own real self. To this erroneous conception that attributes one thing to another (*e. g.*, that *ahankára* is the real self) is due embodied existence—birth, death, old age, sorrow in you, the (reflection of the) *Logos* who is consciousness and is bliss.

309. There is no other (cause) of this changeful existence of you (the reflection of) the *chidatma* (*Logos*) who is unchangeable bliss itself, and whose only form is reality, of stainless glory, than this erroneous conception (that *ahankára* is the real self.)

310. Therefore having, with the great sword of real knowedge, cut down this *ahankăra*, the enemy of the true self—and perceived (to be) like the thorn in the eater's throat, enjoy to heart's content the clearly manifest bliss of the empire of self.

311. Therefore having put an end to the functions of the *ahankára* and the rest, and being free from attachment by the attainment of the supreme object, be happy in the enjoyment of spiritual bliss, and remain silent in Brahm by reaching the all-pervading *logos* and losing all sense of separateness.

312. The great *ahankâra*, even though (apparently) cut down to the roots, will, if excited only for a moment by the mind come to life again and cause a hundred distractions, just as during the rains clouds (are scattered about) by the storm.

313. Having subjugated the enemy *ahankara*, no respite is to be given to it by reflection about objects; such respite is the cause of its revival, just as water is in the case of the extremely weakened lime tree.

314. How can the desirer who exists through the notion of the body being the ego, be the causer of the desire, ohw is (thus) different ? Therefore submission to the pursuit of objects is the cause of bondage, through attachment to differentiations.

315. It is observed that the growth of motive is the growth of the seed (of changing existence), the destruction of the former is the destruction of the latter: therefore the former is to be annihilated.

316. By the strength of *vásaná,** *kárya* (action) is accumulated, and by the accumulation of *kárya, vásaná* increase, (thus) in every way the changeful life of the ego continues.

317. An ascetic must burn out these two, (*vásaná* and *kárya*) in order to sever the bond of changing existence. The growth of *vásaná* is due to these two, thought and external action.

318. *Vásaná*, nourished by these two, produces the changing life of the ego. Means for the destruction of this triad always, under all circumstances (should be sought.)

319. By everywhere, in every way, looking upon everything as Brahm, and by strengthening the perception of the (one) reality this triad will disappear.

320. By the extinction of action,† comes the extinction of anxious thought, from this (latter) the extinction of *vasana*. The final extinction of *vásaná* is liberation—that is also called *jivan mukti*.

321. Aspiration towards the real being fully manifested, *vásaná* as directed to *ahankára* and the rest disappears, as darkness does in the light of the supremely brilliant sun.

322. As on the rising of the sun darkness and the effects of darkness—that net of evils—are not seen, so on the realization of absolute bliss, there is neither bondage nor any trace of pain.

---

* *Vásaná*; an impression remaining unconsciously in the mind from past, good or evil Karma.

† Absolute detachment of the self from action. See *Bhagavad Gita*, ch. iii.

323. Transcending all perceptible objects, realizing the only truth which is full of bliss, controlling the external and internal (organs), so you should pass the time while the bondage of Karma remains.

324. In devotion to Brahm there must be no negligence, Brahma's son* has said that negligence is death.

325. For the wise there is no other danger than negligence in regard to the real form of self. From that springs delusion from delusion *ahankára* from *ahankára* bondage, and from bondage pain.

326. Forgetfulness (of his true self) casts (into the ocean of births and deaths) even a learned man attracted by sense-objects, his mind being perverted, as a woman (casts off) her lover.

327. As moss (covering a sheet of water) does not remain (when pushed back) (fixed) even for a moment, so illusion *(maya)* veils even the learned who turn back (forgetting the real self.

328. If the thinking ego loses its aim and becomes even slightly diverted, then it falls away from the right direction like a playing-ball carelessly dropped on a flight of steps.

329. The mind directed towards objects of sense determines their qualities (and thus becomes attracted by them), from this determination arises desire, and from desire human action.†

330. From that comes separation from the real self; one thus separated retrogrades. There is never seen the reascent but the destruction of the fallen one.

331. Therefore for one possessed of discrimination, knowing Brahm in *samadhi,* there is no death other than from negligence. He who is absorbed in (the real) self, achieves the fullest success; hence be heedful and self-controlled.

---

* Sanat Sujáta says in the *Sanat Sujatiyam* Mahăbhárata. Udyog P. :—"I verily call heedlessness death, and likewise I call freedom from heedlessness immortality." Telang's trans.

† Cf. Bhagavad Gita, ii. 62, 63.

332. Therefore abandon thoughts (about sense-objects), the cause of all evils. He who while living realizes unity (with the supreme), does so also when devoid of the body. For him who is conscious of even the slightest differentiation there is fear—so says the Yajur Veda.*

333. When at any time the learned man perceives even an atom of differentiation in the infinite Brahm, then what is perceived as difference through negligence is to him a (cause of) fear.

334. He who regards what is perceived as the ego, in spite of hundreds of injunctions to the contrary in *Sruti* (Vedas), *Smriti* (law books), and *Nyaya* (logic), falls into a multitude of sorrows on sorrows; (such a man) the doer of what is forbidden, is like a *malimluch* (a demon).

335. The liberated man devoted to the pursuit of truth, always attains the glory of (the real) self, while he who is devoted to the pursuit of the falsehood perishes; this is seen even in the case of a thief and an honest man.

336. The ascetic abandoning the pursuit of unreality, the cause of bondage, rests in the spiritual perception, "I am the Logos." Devotion to Brahm gives bliss through realization of (the real) self and takes away the great pain experienced as the effect of *avidya*.

337. Pursuit of external objects results in increasing evil *vásaná* more and more; therefore realizing the true character of such objects through discriminative knowledge, and abandoning them, be constantly engaged in the pursuit of the real self.

338. The (pursuit of) external objects being checked, tranquillity of the mind *(manas)* is produced; from the tranquillity of *manas* arises the vision of Paramátma (the Logos); from the clear perception of Paramátma (results) the destruction of the bondage of conditioned existence. Restraint of the external is the way to liberation.

---

* *Katha Upanishad.*

339. What learned man, capable of discrimination between the real and the unreal, understanding the supreme object according to the conclusions of the Sruti, and aspiring for liberation, would, like a child, rest in the unreal, the cause of his own fall?

340. There is no *moksha* for him who is attached to body and the rest; in the liberated there is no notion of the body and the rest being the ego. The sleeping man is not awake, and the man awake is not asleep—different attributes inhering in each (condition).

341. He is liberated, who, having (by spiritual intelligence) perceived the Logos within and without, in moveable and immoveable (things), realizing it as the basis of the ego and abandoning all *upádhis*, remains as the all-pervading indestructible Logos.

342. There is no other means for the removal of bondage than the realization of the nature of the Logos. When objects of sense are not pursued, the state of being of the Logos is attained through unremitting devotion to it.

343. How can the non-pursuit of objects of sense which can only with effort be accomplished by the wise, who know the truth, ceaselessly devoted to the Logos, aspiring for eternal bliss, and who have renounced all objects of *dharma* (customary observances) and *karma*(religious rites and ceremonies), be possible to one who regards the body as the self, whose mind is engaged in the pursuit of external objects, and who performs all actions connected with them?

344. For the attainment (of the state of) the Logos by the *Bhikshu*,* engaged in the study of philosophy, *samadhi* is enjoined by the Sruti-text—"Possessed of control over external organs and mind;" and so forth.†

345. Even the wise are not able at once to cause the destruction of egoism which has become strong by growth.

---

* One in fourth stage or *âsrama* of life, a mendicant.

† From the *Brihadáranyaka Upanishad* (See *supra*, xl. 20 *et seq.*)

Except in those who are fixed in *Nirvikalpa samádhi, vásaná* (creates) many births.

346. *Vikshepa sakti,* binding a man to the delusive idea of self through the power of *Avarana sakti,** carries him (into embodied existence) by its qualities.

347. Until the *Avarana sakti* ceases completely, the conquest of the *Vikshepa sakti* is impossible. From its inherent nature the former is destroyed in the self when subject and object are distinguished, as (one distinguishes) milk and water.

348. When there is a complete cessation of the (activity of) the *Vikshepa sakti* in regard to the unreal, then without doubt or impediment arises perfect discrimation, born of clear perception, dividing the real and unreal principles, cutting asunder the bond of delusion produced by *Máyá,* for one emancipated from that there is no more changeful existence.

349. The fire of the knowledge of the oneness (of Brahm) without limitation, burns down completely the forest of *avidyá*; where then is the seed of changeful existence of him who has completely attained the state of oneness?

350. By the thorough realization of the (one) substance *Avarana sakti* ceases. The destruction of false knowledge is the cessation of the pain (arising from) the *Vikshepa sakti.*

351. By the perception of the true character of the rope these three are seen.† Therefore by the wise the essential substance is to be known for the sake of liberation from bondage.

352. Buddhi in conjunction with consciousness,—similar to the union of iron and fire—manifests itself as the faculties of sensation. The effect of this (manifestation) are the three (mentioned above); wherefore what is perceived in error, in dream, and in desire, is false.

---

* *Avarana sakti* is the power that makes one thing appear as another. Vide Sloka 115.

† The power that envelopes the rope as the serpent, the mental perturbation caused thereby, and the erroneous knowledge that the rope is the serpent, are, all three of them, seen to disappear when it is perceived that the rope is the rope and not the serpent.

353. Therefore all these objects beginning with *ahankara*, and ending in the body, are the modifications of Prakriti. These are unreal, because every moment they appear different whereas the atma is at no time otherwise.

354. Paramatma is the eternal, unmixed bliss, the eternal, non-dual, indestructible consciousness, ever the same form, the witness of *buddhi* and the rest, different from both ego and non-ego, its true significance is indicated by the meaning of the word 'I' (*aham*), the real self.

355. The wise man, having thus discriminated between ego non-ego, having ascertained the one reality by innate (spiritual) perception, having realized his own atma as indestructible knowledge, rests in the real self, being free from the two (ego and non-ego).

356. When by *avikalpa samadhi* the non-dual atma is realised, then is ignorance—the knot of the heart—completely destroyed.

357. Paramatma (the Logos), being non-dual and without difference, such conceptions as I, thou, and this, are produced through the defects of *buddhi*. But when *samadhi* is manifest, all differentiation connected with him (the *jiva*) becomes destroyed through the realization of the (one) real substance.

358. The ascetic possessed of *sama*, *dama*, supreme *uparati* and *kshánati* (endurance), and devoted to *samadhi*, perceives the state of the Logos, and through that (perception) completely burns down all *vikalpa* (error) produced by *avidya* and dwells in bliss in Brahm free from *vikalpa* and action.

359. Those alone are freed from the bondage of conditioned being who, having transcended all externals, such as hearing, mind, self and egotism in the *chidàtma*, (the Logos), are absorbed in it, not those who simply speak about the mystery.

360. Through the differences of *upadhi*, the true self seems to be divided, on the removal of *upadhi* the one true self remains. Therefore let the wise man remain always devoted to *Akalpa samâdhi* until the final dissolution or *upadhi*.

361. The man, devoted to *sat* (the real), becomes *sat* through exclusive devotion to that one. (As) the insect thinking constantly of the humble-bee becomes itself the bee.*

362. The insect, abandoning attachment to all other action, meditating on that humble-bee, attains the state of the humble-bee. Similarly the yogi meditating on the Paramatma (Logos), becomes it through devotion to that one.

363. The excessively subtile Paramatma (the Logos) cannot be perceived through the gross vision. (It is) to be known by worthy men, with very pure *búddhi* through the *samádhi* and supremely subtile (spiritual) faculties.

364. As gold, properly purified by fire, attains its essential quality, abandoning all dross; so the *Manas*, abandoning the impurities *satva*, *rajas*, and *tamas* through meditation attains the Supreme Reality.

365. When the *Manas*, matured by ceaseless discipline of this kind, becomes merged in Brahm, then *samádhi*, devoid of all *vikalpa* (differences such as between subject and object), becomes of itself the producer of the realization of non-dual bliss.

366. By this *samádhi* there is destruction of the entire knot of *vásaná* (desires), and (there is) extinction of all *karma* (action). So there is always and in every way, within and without, a spontaneous manifestation of *Svarupa* (Logos).

367. Know meditation to be a hundred times (superior) to listening, assimilation to be hundred thousand times (superior) to meditation, and *Nirvikalpa Samadhi* to be infinitely (superior) to assimilation.

---

* It is usually believed in India that a cockroach, shut up with a humble-bee, becomes after a time changed into the latter. A writer in this magazine states that he has witnessed such a transformation. (See *Theosophist*, vol. vi). The phenomenon in question is unknown to modern entomologists. It seems desirable that very careful and repeated observations should be made to determine the matter. Of course the statement in the text is but an illustration and not an argument; and it is quite independent of the genuineness of the phenomenon.

368. Verily by *Nirvikalpa Samádhi* the essential reality called Brahm is clearly realized : not by any other means. (As the non-dual reality) becomes mixed with other conceptions through the inconstancy of the activities of the *Manas*.

369. Therefore with the organs of sense restrained, and in uninterrupted tranquility of mind, be engaged in meditation on the logos; and by perception of one reality, destroy the darkness caused by beginningless *avidyá*.

370. The first gate of yoga is the control of speech, then non-acceptance (of anything and all), absence of expectation, absence of desire and uninterrupted devotion to the one (reality).

371. Uninterrupted devotion to the one (reality) is the cause of the cessation of sense-enjoyment, *dama* is the cause of the tranquillity of the thinking self, and on account of *sama* egotism is dissolved. Thence proceeds the yogi's perpetual enjoyment of the bliss of Brahm. Therefore the cessation of the activity of the thinking self is to be attained with effort by the ascetic.

372. Control speech by (thy) self, and that by *buddhi* (intellect) ; and *búddhi* by the witness of *buddhi* (divine light), merge that in *Nirvikalpa purnatma* (the Logos where no distinction exists between ego and non-ego) and obtain supreme rest.

373. The yogi attains the state of those *upadhis*, viz., body, life principle, senses, mind, intellect, etc., with whose functions he is engaged (for the time being).

374. It is observed that on the cessation of activity (of those functions and *upadhis*), there comes for the *Muni* that perfect happiness which is caused by abstinence from the pleasures of the senses and the realization of eternal bliss.

375. Renunciation, external and internal, is fit only for him who is dispassionate. Therefore the dispassionate man on account of the aspiration for liberation forsakes all attachment, whether internal or external.

376. External attachment is to objects of sense, internal is to egotism and the rest. It is only the dispassionate man, devoted to Brahm, who is able to renounce them.

377. O thou, discriminating man! Know renunciation and spiritual knowledge to be the two wings of the embodied ego. By nothing other than these two can ascent to the top of the creeper of nectar called liberation be accomplished.

378. For him who is possessed of excessive dispassion there is *samádhi*; for him in *samádhi* there is unwavering spiritual perception. For him who has perceived the essential reality there is liberation, and for the liberated atma there is realization of eternal bliss.

379. For one whose self is controlled, I see no better generator of happiness than dispassion. If that, again, is accompanied by clear spiritual perception, he becomes the enjoyer of the empire of self-dominion; this is the permanent gate of the maiden (named) liberation. Therefore thou who art different from this, being void of attachment to everything, ever gain knowledge of (thy) self for the sake of liberation.

380. Cut off desire of objects of sense which are like poison these are the causes of death. Having forsaken selfish attachment to caste, family and religious order, renounce all acts proceeding from attachment. Abandon the notion of self in regard to unreality—body and the rest—and gain knowledge of self. In reality thou art the seer, stainless, and (the manifestation of) the supreme non-dual Brahm.

381. Having firmly applied the *manas* to the goal, Brahm, having confined the external organs to their own places, with the body motionless, regardless of its state or condition, and having realized the unity of the atma and Brahm by absorption, and abiding in the indestructible, always and abundantly drink in the essence of Brahmic bliss in thyself. What is the use of all else which is void of happiness?

382. Abandoning all thought of not-spirit, which stains the mind and is the cause of suffering, think of átmá, which is bliss and which is the cause of liberation.

383. (This átmá) is self illuminating, the witness of all (objects) and is ever manifest in the *Vignánamaya Kosha* Making this, which is different from *asat* (unreal), the aim, realize it as the indestructible self by abiding in it.

384. Uttering its name, realize it clearly as the essential form of self, the indivisible being, not dependent upon another.

385. Thoroughly realising it as the self, and giving up the idea of self as being egotism and the rest, and yet remaining in them, (regard them) as broken earthen-pots through want of interest in them.*

386. Having applied the purified *antah karna* (the *mind*) to the real self, which is the witness, the absolute knowledge, leading it by slow degrees to steadiness, realize the *Purn-atma*.

387. Regard the indestructible and all-pervading atma, freed from all the *upadhis*—body, senses, vitality, mind, egotism and the rest—produced by ignorance as *mahá akasha* (great space).

388. As space, freed from a hundred *upadhis* (such as) the small and large earthen pots, containing rice and other grains, is one and not many, similarly the pure Supreme, freed from egotism and the rest, is but one.

389. From Brahm down to the post, all *upadhis* are merely illusive. Therefore realize the all-pervading atma as one and the same.

390 Whatever is imagined through error as different (from the real), is not so on right perception, but it is merely that (thing itself) On the cessation of error what was seen before as a snake appears as the rope, similarly the universe is in reality the atma.

---

* Have no more concern than people have about such worthless things as broken pots, which the ordinary Hindu house-holder looks upon as inauspicious objects not fit to be kept in any prominent part of the house.

391. The atma is Brahma, the atma is Vishnu, the atma is Indra, the atma is Siva, the atma is the whole of this universe; besides atma there is nothing.

392. The atma is within, the atma is without, the atma is before; the atma is behind, the atma is in the south, the atma, is in the north, the atma is also above and below.

393. As wave, foam, whirlpool and bubble—are all essentially but water, so all, beginning with the body and ending with egotism, and but consciousness, which is pure are absolute happiness.

394. Verily all this universe, known through mind and speech, is the spirit; verily nothing is except the spirit which lies on the other side of Prakriti. Are the various kinds of earthen-vessels different from the earth? The embodied ego, deluded by the wine of Maya, speaks of 'I' and 'you.'

395. By the cessation of action there remains no other than this. The Sruti declares the absence of duality, for the purpose of removing the erroneous conception that attributes one thing to another.

396. The real self is (in essence) the Supreme Brahm, pure as space, void of *vikalpa*, of boundary, of motion, of modification, of within and without, the secondless, having no other, (so) what else is there to know?

397. What more is there to say? *Jiva* (ego), *swayam*, (the real self), from the atom to the Universe, all is the non-dual Brahm—in different forms; the Sruti says: I (the Logos) am Parabrahm. Those whose minds are thus illuminated, having abandoned all externals, abide in the eternal *Chidananda Atma* (the Logos which is consciousness and bliss) and thus reach Brahm. This is quite certain.

398. Kill out by the force (of Will) desires raised through egoism in the physical body full of filth, then those raised in the astral body which is like air. Know the (real) self, whose glory is celebrated in the Vedas, to be eternal, very bliss, and remain in Brahm.

t

399. So long as a man is attached to the corpse-form,* he is impure† through enemies,‡ there is suffering associated with birth, death and disease. When he perceives the pure atma which is bliss and is immoveable, then only (he) becomes free from these—so the Vedas declare.

400. On the removal of all phenomenal attributes imposed upon the self, the true self is (found to be) the supreme, non-dual, all pervading and actionless Brahm.

401. When the functions of the thinking self are at rest in Paratma (the Logos), which is (in essence) Parabrahm void of *vikalpa,* then this *vikalpa* is perceived no longer and mere wild talk remains.

402. In the one substance, undifferentiable, formless and devoid of *visesha*§ where is there difference? Hence the distinction that this is the universe, is a false conception.

403. In the one substance, devoid of the conditions (of being), such as knower, knowledge and known, and undifferentiable, formless and devoid of *visesha,* where is there difference?

404. In the one substance, full as the ocean of *Kalpa,*‖ and undifferentiable, formless, and devoid of *visesha,* where is the difference?

405. In the supreme reality, secondless and devoid of *visesha,* in which ignorance the cause of illusion is destroyed, as darkness is in light, where is the difference?

406. In the one supreme reality, how can there be any indication of difference? By whom has any difference been perceived in *sushupti,* which is merely a state of happiness.

407. On the realization of the supreme Truth, in none of the three divisions of time is there the universe in *sadatma* (the real self), which is (in substance) Brahm, void of *vikalpa* (distinction or duality). (As on the truth being

---

* *i.e.,* the physical body.

† In a Levitical sense.

‡ *i.e.,* the six passions, lust, anger, greed, delusion, pride and jealousy.

§ The distinctness of one object from another.

‖ Ocean = the supremely subtle cause into which everything returns at the universal *pralaya.*

perceived) there is no snake in the rope nor a drop of water in the mirage*.

408. This quality exists only through *Maya*, in absolute reality there is no quality; this the Vedas say clearly and it is perceived in *sushupti*.

409. The identity of that which is attributed to the substance with the substance itself has been perceived by the wise in the case of the rope and serpent. The distinction is kept alive by error.

410. This distinction has its root in the thinking principle; without the thinking principle it does not exist. Therefore bring the thinking principle to rest in *Paramatma* which is the Logos.

411. The wise man in *samadhi* perceives in his heart (that something which is eternal knowledge, pure bliss, the supreme limit incomparable, eternally free, actionless, as limitless as space, stainless, without distinction of subject and object, and is the all-pervading Brahm (in essence.)

412. The wise man in *samadhi* perceives in his heart (that something) which is devoid of Prakriti and its modifications, whose state or being is beyond (our) conception and which is uniform, unequalled, beyond the knot of *manas*, established by the declarations of the Vedas, and known as the eternal Logos, and is the all pervading Brahm (in essence).

413. The wise man in *samadhi* perceives in his heart the undecaying, immortal substance, which is like a motionless ocean not indicated by mere negation, without name, in whom the activity of the *gunas* is at an end, eternal, peaceful and one.

414. Having brought the *antahkarana* (mind) to rest, in the true self, you should perceive it, whose glory is indestructible; with assiduous efforts sever the bondage tainted by the smell of conditioned existence, and render fruitful your manhood.

* In which they had been perceived erroneously.

415. Realize the atma existing in yourself, freed from all *upadhis*, the non-dual being, consciousness, and bliss, and you will no longer be subject to evolution.

416. The *Mahatma* having (once) abandoned the visible body as if it was a corpse—the body which, through experiencing the effects of Karma, is regarded as a reflected shadow of the man—does not again fix his thoughts upon it.

417. Having approached the Logos which is eternal, pure knowledge and bliss, abandon this *upadhi* (the body) which is impure. Then it is not to be thought of again, the recollection of what is vomited is only calculated to disgust.

418. The great wise man having burnt all this down to the roots in the fire of the real self, which is the non-dual Brahm in essence, remains in the Logos, which is eternal, pure knowledge and bliss.

419. The knower of truth, whose being is (gradually) being absorbed into the Logos, which is bliss, and Brahm, does not again look at the body, strung on the thread of *prarabdha** *Karma* and (unholy) as cow's blood—whether the body remains or disappears.

420. Having perceived the Logos which is indestructible and the knower of truth nourish the body?

421. The gain of the yogi who has attained perfection and is a Jivanmukta is the employment of perpetual bliss in the atma who is within and without.

422. The result of dispassion is right perception; of right perception, abstention from the pleasures of sense and ceremonial acts. The peace that comes from the realization of the bliss of self is the fruit of abstention from ceremonial acts, from the pleasures of sense.

423. The absence of what follows (in the order given above) renders fruitless the one that precedes it. Perfect satisfaction proceeding from the unparalleled bliss that comes from self is liberation.

---

* Latent possibilities which have become dynamic,

424. The fruit of wisdom is declared to be freedom from anxiety at the sight of trouble. How can a man of right discrimination do afterwards* the blameworthy acts done when deluded ?

425. It is perceived that the fruit of wisdom is liberation from *asat* (*Prakriti*), that of ignorance is attachment to it. If this (difference) is not perceived between the ignorant and the wise, as in the mirage, etc, where can we see any gain for the wise ?

426. If the knot of the heart,† ignorance, is entirely destroyed, then how can objects by themselves be the cause of attachment in repect of one who is without desires ?

427. The non-appearance of even conscious inclination towards objects of enjoyment is the extreme limit of dispassion ; the nonevolution of egotism is the supreme limit of right discrimination ; the non-evolution of self-conscious being by absorption in the Logos, is the extreme limit of *uparati*.‡

428. He on this earth is happy and worthy of honour who, by always resting in peace in the form of Brahm, is freed from external consciousness, regarding the objects of enjoyment experienced by others as a sleeping child (would do), looking upon the universe as the world perceived in dream, at times recovers consciousness and enjoys the fruit of an infinity of meritorious deeds.

429. This ascetic, firm in wisdom, free from changes of condition, actionless, enjoys perpetual bliss, his atma being absorbed in Brahm.

430. *Pragna* or wisdom is said to be that state of ideation which recognises no such distinction as that of ego and non-ego, and which is absorbed in the manifested unity of Brahm and atma.

---

* *i.e.*, when the illusion is extinguished.

† Between object and subject there is no relation except through illusion, and hence it is looked upon as a knot tying together the ego and non-ego.

‡ Peace, tranquillity. See sl. 24.

431. He who is perfectly at rest (in this wisdom) is said to be firm in wisdom. He who is firm in wisdom, whose bliss is uninterrupted and by whom the objective universe is well-nigh forgotten, is regarded as *jivanmukta.*

432. He is regarded as *jivanmukta* who, though having his consciousness absorbed (in the Logos), is awake and yet devoid of all characteristics of waking, whose consciousness it free from even unconscious traces of desire.

433. He is regarded as *jivanmukta* in whom all tendency to evolution is at rest, who though possessed of *kala* (ray of the Logos), is yet devoid of it (from the standpoint of Brahm), whose thinking principle is devoid of thinking.

434. Though existing in this body which is like a shadow to be yet devoid of egotism and the consciousness of possession,* is the characteristic of a *jivanmukta.*

435. Want of inquiry into the past, absence of speculation about the future, and indifference (as to the present), are the characteristics of a *jivanmukta.*

436. By nature (from acquired natural disposition) to regard all as equal everywhere in this world of opposites, full as of good and bad qnalities, is the characterstic of a *jivanmukta.*

437. On meeting with objects, agreeable and disagreeable, to regard them all as equal in (respect to) oneself and to feel no perturbation in either case, is characterstic of a *jivanmukta.*

438. The absence of external and internal perception in the ascetic by reason of his consciousness being centred in the enjoyment of Brahmic bliss, is characterstic of a *jivanmukta.*

439. He who is free from egotism and 'my-ness' in what is done by body, senses, etc., and who remains indifferent, is possessed of the characterstic of a *jivanmukta.*

440. He who has realized the identity of Atma with Brahm by the power of Vedic wisdom and is freed from the bondage of conditioned existence, is possessed of the characterstic of a *jivanmukta.*

---

* Literally my-ne.

441. He in whom the consciousness of *I* in regard to the body and organs, and of *this* in regard to other subjects, never arises, is considered a *jivanmukta.*

442. He who, by reason of wisdom, knows there is no difference between *Pratyagatma* (Logos) and Brahma, as also between Brahm and the universe, is possessed of the characteristic of a *jivanmukta.*

443. He who is the same, whether worshipped by the good or harassed by the wicked, is possessed of the characterstic of a *jivanmukta.*

444 The ascetic, into whom (into whose consciousness) enter and become merged objects called into existence by *Para* (light of the Logos) as the rivers flow into the ocean by reason of his being nothing but *sat* (because Parabrahm), and do not produce any change, is liberated.

445. For him who has gained the true knowledge of Brahma there is no more evolution as before: if there be these the Brahmic state is not known (he is out of it.)

446. If it is said 'he evolves through the force of previous *vásaná'*—it is not so, *Vásaná** becomes powerless by the realizasion of identity with the Reality.

447 As the tendency of the most lustful man ceases before his mother, so (the *vásaná*) of the wise ceases on knowing Brahm, the perfect bliss.

448. Dependence on (external) objects is seen in one engaged in deep meditation on account of the results of Karma already in operation—so say the Vedas.

499. So long as there is perception of pain and pleasure, so long *Prâravdha* exists; these results are preceded by Karma for one devoid of Karma they connot be anywhere.

450 By the knowledge that I (the Logos) am Brahm, the Karma acquired in a thousand millions of kalpas is extinguished, as is the Karma of dream life on awaking.

450 Whatever is done, whether manifestly good or bad in dreams—how is it (efficacious) for the going to heaven or hell of the dreamer awakened?

† Impressions remaining unconsciously in the mind from past Karma.

CHARAPATAPANJARI

OF

Srimat Sankaracharya translatedby J. N. Parmanand.

I salute the glorious Ganesh. Worship god, Oh foolish man, worship god. When death approaches, the study of grammar will not save you. The child is absorbed in play, the young man is attached to the young woman, the old man is lost in anxiety, and none devotes himself to the Great Brahma. Worship &c. 2.

The body has become impaired, the head heavy, and the mouth toothless, the old man goes stick in hand, yet hope does not leave him. Worship &c. 3.

(Dead) persons are born again and die again and again lie in the wombs of their mothers or this insurmountable world; save me, Oh Lord by Your Grace, take me to the opposite shore Worship &c. 4.

Day and night, morning and evening, winter and spring come round (in succession); time passes on and life is spent but hope does not leave man. Worship &c. 5.

Man keeps clotted hair or shaves his head bald, puts on dress of a reddish colour; he sees and is yet blind and disguises himself variously for the sake of his belly. Worship &c. 6.

Where is passion when youth is gone, what is the lake when its water dries up, where is the band of dependents when wealth is exhausted, and what is the world when the reality is known. Worship &c. 7.

In his front is fire, on the back sun-shine, at night he puts his knees to his chest, he begs and lives beneath a tree, yet desires do not leave him. Worship &c. 8.

So long as he is engaged in earning money his dependents affectionately follow him; when he becomes disabled in body he is not cared for at home. Worship &c. 9.

It is (like) a sheet of rags joined together; a path in which merit and demerit are alike neglected. There is neither you nor I nor a third person, why then are you aggrieved. Worship &c. 10.

On seeing the breasts and hips of women you fondly become attached to them, but consider constantly that they are merely forms of flesh, fat &c. Worship &c. 11.

The Gita should be sung, the almighty should be constantly meditated upon, the mind should be devoted to the company of the good, and money should be given to the poor. Worship &c. 12.

Whoever has studied the Gita a little, has drunk a particle of the waters of the Ganges, and has worshipped god, him does Yama investigate into (? his conduct)? Worship &c., 13.

Who am I, who are you, whence have you come, who is my mother, who is my father. Leaving aside all unreal dreams consider this. Worship &c. 14.

Who is your wife, who is your son, this world is very curious whence have you come; Oh brother consider the reality in your mind. Worship &c. 15.

One's habitation should be the foot of a tree on the banks of the Ganges, bed the surface of the earth, clothes a deerskins all objects of enjoyment should be abandoned; to whom does such abandonment of the world not give happiness. Worship.